BIBLICA ET ORIENTALIA
(SACRA SCRIPTURA ANTIQUITATIBUS ORIENTALIBUS ILLUSTRATA)
26

ROMAE
E PONTIFICIO INSTITUTO BIBLICO
1973

KEVIN J. CATHCART
UNIVERSITY OF OTTAWA

NAHUM IN THE LIGHT OF NORTHWEST SEMITIC

ROME
BIBLICAL INSTITUTE PRESS
1973

TYPIS PONTIFICIAE UNIVERSITATIS GREGORIANAE — ROMAE

Preface

The present study was submitted in a slightly different form to the Oriental Faculty of the Pontifical Biblical Institute, Rome, in partial fulfilment of the requirements for the degree of Doctor of Ancient Oriental Studies. I would like to express my sincere thanks to Rev. Mitchell Dahood, S.J., for his expert guidance and constant interest and encouragement, when the work was in progress. I am also indebted to Rev. R. Caplice, S.J., Rev. A. Cody, O.S.B., and Rev. J. J. A. van Dijk, who read the original dissertation and made a number of invaluable suggestions. The final draft of the work is my own and I am entirely responsible for any weaknesses therein.

I would like to thank Rev. C. Martini, S.J., Rector of the Pontifical Biblical Institute, and Rev. Stanislas Lyonnet, S.J., editor, for accepting this work into the series "Biblica et Orientalia". My special thanks go to Rev. James Swetnam, S.J., the managing editor of the series, who guided this book through its actual production.

My pursuit of Oriental studies could never have been sustained without the constant affection, interest, and encouragement that I received from my parents. Lastly I dedicate this work to my wife Ann, whose loving contribution in this endeavour could never be adequately expressed in words.

Ottawa, Canada

Kevin J. Cathcart

TABLE OF CONTENTS

Abbreviations

1. Publications

AfO . . . . . . *Archiv für Orientforschung*
AHw . . . . . *Akkadisches Handwörterbuch*, by W. von Soden
AIS . . . . . . *The Aramaic Inscriptions of Sefîre*, by J. A. Fitzmyer
AJSL . . . . . *American Journal of Semitic Languages and Literatures*
ANES . . . . . *Journal of the Ancient Near Eastern Society of Columbia University*
ANET . . . . *Ancient Near Eastern Texts*, edited by J. B. Pritchard
ARM . . . . . Archives Royales de Mari, edited by A. Parrot and G. Dossin
ATD. . . . . . Das Alte Testament Deutsch
BA . . . . . . *Biblical Archaeologist*
BANE . . . . *The Bible and the Ancient Near East*, edited by G. E. Wright
BASOR . . . . *Bulletin of the American Schools of Oriental Research*
BCCT . . . . . *The Bible in Current Catholic Thought*, edited by J. L. McKenzie
BDB. . . . . . F. Brown, S. R. Driver, and C. A. Briggs, ed., *A Hebrew and English Lexicon of the Old Testament*
*BH*³ . . . . . . *Biblia Hebraica*, edited by R. Kittel, 3rd edition
BJ . . . . . . Bible de Jérusalem. *La Sainte Bible*, traduite en français ... sous la direction de l'École Biblique de Jérusalem
BL . . . . . . H. Bauer and P. Leander, *Historische Grammatik der hebräischen Sprache*
BO . . . . . . *Bibliotheca Orientalis*
BZ . . . . . . *Biblische Zeitschrift*
BZAW . . . . Beihefte zur Zeitschrift für die alttestamentliche Wissenschaft
CAD. . . . . . *The Assyrian Dictionary* of the Oriental Institute of the University of Chicago
CBQ . . . . . *Catholic Biblical Quarterly*
CECBN . . . . *A Critical and Exegetical Commentary on the Book of Nahum*, by J. M. P. Smith
CIG . . . . . . *Corpus Inscriptionum Graecarum*
CIL . . . . . . *Corpus Inscriptionum Latinarum*
CIS . . . . . . *Corpus Inscriptionum Semiticarum*
CML . . . . . *Canaanite Myths and Legends*, by G. R. Driver
DISO . . . . . *Dictionnaire des inscriptions sémitiques de l'Ouest*, by C. F. Jean and J. Hoftijzer
EA . . . . . . *Die El-Amarna Tafeln*, edited by J. A. Knudtzon

ETL.	*Ephemerides Theologicae Lovanienses*
FuF	*Forschungen und Fortschritte*
GB	W. Gesenius, and F. Buhl, *Hebräisches und aramäisches Handwörterbuch über das Alte Testament*
GHB.	*Grammaire de l'hébreu biblique*, by P. Joüon
GK	W. Gesenius, and E. Kautzsch, *Gesenius' Hebrew Grammar*, translated by A. E. Cowley
HALAT	*Hebräisches und aramäisches Lexikon zum Alten Testament*, by W. Baumgartner with B. Hartmann and E. Y. Kutscher
HAT.	Handbuch zum Alten Testament
HKAT	Handkommentar zum Alten Testament
HSAT	Die Heilige Schrift des Alten Testament
HTR	*Harvard Theological Review*
HUCA.	*Hebrew Union College Annual*
ICC	The International Critical Commentary
IDB	*Interpreter's Dictionary of the Bible*
IEJ	*Israel Exploration Journal*
JAOS	*Journal of the Americal Oriental Society*
JBL	*Journal of Biblical Literature*
JCS	*Journal of Cuneiform Studies*
JJS	*Journal of Jewish Studies*
JNES	*Journal of Near Eastern Studies*
JPOS	*Journal of the Palestine Oriental Society*
JQR	*Jewish Quarterly Review*
JSS	*Journal of Semitic Studies*
JTS	*Journal of Theological Studies*
KAI.	*Kanaanäische und aramäische Inschriften*, by H. Donner and W. Röllig
KB	L. Köhler and W. Baumgartner, *Lexicon in Veteris Testamenti Libros*
KHC	Kurzer Hand-Commentar zum Alten Testament
KJ	The Authorized Version of 1611, or the King James Version
LKK	*Legend of King Keret*, by H. L. Ginsberg
NEB	*The New English Bible*, 1970
OLZ	*Orientalistische Literaturzeitung*
PEQ.	*Palestine Exploration Quarterly*
PG	Patrologia Graeca, edited by J. P. Migne
PL	Patrologia Latina, edited by J. P. Migne
PNWSP	*Proverbs and Northwest Semitic Philology*, by M. Dahood
PSID	*The Proto-Sinaitic Inscriptions and their Decipherment*, by W. F. Albright
4QpNah	Pesher of Nahum
RB	*Revue biblique*
REJ	*Revue des études juives*
RHR	*Revue de l'histoire des religions*
RSV.	*Revised Standard Version*, 1946, 1952.
UHP	*Ugaritic–Hebrew Philology*, by M. Dahood

UT	*Ugaritic Textbook*, 4th edition 1965 of C. H. Gordon's *Ugaritic Grammar*
VT	*Vetus Testamentum*
VTS	Supplements to *Vetus Testamentum*
WuS.	*Wörterbuch der ugaritischen Sprache*, by J. Aistleitner
ZAW	*Zeitschrift für die alttestamentliche Wissenschaft*
ZDMG.	*Zeitschrift der deutschen morgenländischen Gesellschaft*
ZLH.	F. Zorell, *Lexicon Hebraicum et Aramaicum Veteris Testamenti*

2. Other Abbreviations

Akk.	Akkadian
Ar.	Arabic
Aram.	Aramaic
Eth.	Ethiopic
Heb.	Hebrew
LXX	The Septuagint
MT	Massoretic Text
Phoen.	Phoenician
Sum.	Sumerian
Symm.	Ancient Greek translation of the Old Testament by Symmachus
Targ.	Targum
Ugar.	Ugaritic
VL	Vetus Latina
Vulg.	The Vulgate

The older standard commentaries on Nahum are cited usually by the name of the author only ; full reference may be found in the bibliography.

Introduction

Some years after G. Bickell (1) and H. Gunkel (2) had made their reconstructions of the first chapter of the Book of Nahum, W. R. Arnold protested to the academic world that those scholars had " decapitated a masterpiece of Hebrew Literature ". (3) Although recent critics have not been as drastic as their predecessors in their handling of the text, most of them still resort to emendations, transpositions and even excisions to clear up problems or to restore what they consider to be the original text. One commentator warns his readers that in the Book of Nahum they have " a seriously corrupt text in Ch. 1 ; but for Chs 2 – 3, although editors have made some twenty minor additions, and although in the course of centuries numerous mistakes in copying have occurred, fortunately the original poem in the main is recoverable ". (4)

(1) " Die hebräische Metrik ", *ZDMG* 34 (1880) 559-560 ; *idem*, *Carmina Veteris Testamenti Metrice* (Innsbruck 1882) pp. 211-213 ; *idem*, *Beiträge zur hebräische Metrik I : Das alphabetische Lied in Nahum 1,2 – 2,3* (Sitzungsberichte des phil.-hist. Classe der kaiserlichen Akademie der Wissenschaften, V ; Vienna 1894).

(2) " Nahum 1 ", *ZAW* 13 (1893) 223-244 ; *idem*, *Schöpfung und Chaos* (Göttingen 1895) pp. 102 ff.

(3) " The Composition of Nahum 1 – 2 : 3 ", *ZAW* 21 (1901) 236.

It should be noted of course that Bickell and Gunkel were trying to restore, first, an alleged complete alphabetic acrostic psalm, and, secondly, what they considered to be the correct and original metrical pattern of the poem. F. Delitzsch in his *Biblischer Kommentar über die Psalmen* (Leipzig ; 3rd edition 1873), p. 117, reported how a certain Pastor G. Frohnmeyer had observed the alphabetic character of the introductory psalm in Nahum. It was following this observation that Bickell, Gunkel, Nowack, Happel and van Hoonacker in turn, carried out major critical surgery on the text of Nahum. Other and subsequent critics were not quite so ardent, and few scholars have pursued the acrostic beyond vv. 8, 9 or 10 of Chapter 1. Cf. e.g., O. Eissfeldt, *The Old Testament : An Introduction* (Oxford 1965) p. 414. The note in the *NEB* which says : " Verses 2-14 are an incomplete alphabetic acrostic poem ; some parts have been re-arranged accordingly ", is quite unclear and could be misleading.

(4) C. L. Taylor, " Nahum : Introduction and Exegesis ", *The Interpreter's Bible*, VI (New York 1956) p. 954.

A. Haldar, in his *Studies in the Book of Nahum* (Uppsala 1947), manages to steer away from the course of the emendators, but he does not believe that Nahum can be " interpreted satisfactorily by a purely linguistic method " ([5]), and claims that in his textual and philological study, he had the advantage of working with his religio-historical interpretation of the book. ([6]) A feature of Haldar's work is the considerable attention which he gives to discussion of the ancient versions, but he rarely finds them pointing to a different underlying Hebrew text.

Recently discovered witnesses of the text of Nahum, including the Pesher of Nahum (4QpNah) found at Qumran; ([7]) the Hebrew scroll of the Minor Prophets from Wadi Murabbaʿât, ([8]) and fragments of a Greek text of the Minor Prophets from Naḥal Ḥever, ([9]) indicate that the consonantal text found in the Hebrew Bible today has been handed down with incredible accuracy for nearly two thousand years at least. The absence of many variant readings in 4QpNah will disappoint A. George who a few years ago wrote: " D'ici quelques années sans doute, on pourra disposer pour l'améliorer de témoins anciens : on a signalé la découverte dans la grotte 4 de Qumran d'un texte hébreu de Nahum et d'un pesher du même livre ...". ([10])

([5]) *Studies*, p. 1.

([6]) Haldar's actual interpretation is developed in the second part of his *Studies*. He believes that the Book of Nahum originated in cultic circles and that in it the historical enemy is identified with cosmic foes in Sumerian, Babylonian and Ugaritic mythology.

([7]) The *editio princeps* of 4QpNah is found in J. M. Allegro with the collaboration of A. A. Anderson, *Discoveries in the Judaean Desert V*, *Qumran Cave 4. I (4Q158-4Q186)* (Oxford 1968) pp. 37-42 + plates XII-XIV.

([8]) P. Benoit, J. T. Milik, and R. de Vaux, *Les Grottes de Murabbaʿât : Discoveries in the Judaean Desert II* (Oxford 1961) esp. pp. 197-198 + plates LXVI-LXVII.

([9]) D. Barthélemy, *Les Devanciers d'Aquila : Première publication intégrale du texte des fragments du dodécaprophéton* (VTS 10 ; Leiden 1963) pp. 163-272. For Barthélemy's earlier report, see " Redécouverte d'un chaînon manquant de l'histoire de la Septante ", *RB* 60 (1953) 18-29. See also B. Lifshitz, " The Greek Documents from the Cave of Horror ", *IEJ* 12 (1962) 201-207 ; F. M. Cross, " The History of the Biblical Text in the Light of Discoveries in the Judaean Desert ", *HTR* 57 (1964) 281 ff. ; *idem*, " The Contribution of the Qumran Discoveries to the Study of the Biblical Text ", *IEJ* 16 (1966) 84-85 ; P. W. Skehan, " The Scrolls and the Old Testament Text ", in *New Directions in Biblical Archaeology*, edited by D. N. Freedman and J. C. Greenfield (Garden City, N. Y. 1971) pp. 108 ff.

([10]) " Nahum ", in *Dictionnaire de la Bible : Supplément*, Vol. VI (Paris 1960) Col. 291.

This study attempts to explain many of the " difficulties " in Nahum by utilizing the materials now available as a result of epigraphical discoveries and subsequent advances in the study of comparative Semitic philology and comparative ancient Near Eastern literatures. As Hebrew is a Northwest Semitic language, the scholar must give particular attention to the other languages which belong to that group, especially Ugaritic and Phoenician. The present writer believes that grammatical, syntactical and lexical problems can often be adequately explained by comparative Northwest Semitic philology, thus removing the necessity for " improvement " of the text. To the writer's knowledge, this approach to the study of the Hebrew text of Nahum has not been attempted in a thorough manner. Although Haldar stresses the close relationship between Hebrew and Ugaritic and calls for caution in the use of Arabic to elucidate Biblical Hebrew, (11) the material at his disposal when he made his study, was not as abundant as it is now.

The first part of each chapter presents the Hebrew text with syllable and stress counts and a new translation. The syllable counts constitute what R. C. Culley (12) has called (correctly in our opinion) a descriptive approach to Hebrew metre. The syllable counts in Nahum are so interesting that we believe we have employed a method which, as Culley says, will bring " to light something of the poetic structure " and permit " some distinctions to be made within the corpus of classical Hebrew Poetry ". (13) The second part of each chapter is a philological commentary in which grammatical, syntactical and lexical problems are examined in the light of Northwest Semitic. However, in a number of cases Akkadian or Arabic material has been included where it was found useful. Whenever possible, parallels from other books of the Bible and from ancient Near Eastern literature generally, have been given to support the translation offered. It should be pointed out however that caution has to be exercised in evaluating the significance of these " parallels ". We refer for example to the alleged Mesopotamian influence on Hebrew literature and we endorse the position taken by T. F. McDaniel, (14) who seems to make a very good case for great reservation in dealing with alleged " parallels ".

(11) *Studies*, pp. 7 f.

(12) " Metrical Analysis of Classical Hebrew Poetry ", in *Essays on the Ancient Semitic World*, edited by J. W. Wevers and D. B. Redford (Toronto 1970) p. 4.

(13) *Ibid.*, p. 28.

(14) " The Alleged Sumerian Influence upon Lamentations ", *VT* 18 (1968) 198-209.

Bibliography

Aharoni Y., " Hebrew Ostraca from Tel Arad ", *IEJ* 16 (1966) 1-7.

——, " The Use of Hieratic Numerals in Hebrew Ostraca and the Shekel Weights ", *BASOR* 184 (1966) 13-19.

——, " Arad : Its Inscriptions and Temple ", *BA* 31 (1968) 2-32.

——, " Trial Excavations in the ' Solar Shrine ' at Lachish ", *IEJ* 18 (1968) 157-169.

——, " Three Hebrew Ostraca from Arad ", *BASOR* 197 (1970) 16-42.

Aistleitner J., *Wörterbuch der ugaritischen Sprache* (Berlin 1963).

Albright W. F., " The Seal of Eliakim and the Latest Preexilic History of Judah, with some observations on Ezechiel ", *JBL* 51 (1932) 77-106.

——, " The Song of Deborah in the Light of Archaeology ", *BASOR* 62 (1936) 26-31.

——, " New Canaanite Historical and Mythological Data ", *BASOR* 63 (1936) 23-32.

——, " New Light on the Early History of Phoenician Colonization ", *BASOR* 83 (1941) 14-22.

——, *Archaeology and the Religion of Israel* (Baltimore 1942 ; 2nd edition 1946).

——, " Two Little Understood Amarna Letters from the Middle Jordan Valley," *BASOR* 89 (1943) 7-17.

——, " The Old Testament and Canaanite Language and Literature ", *CBQ* 7 (1945) 5-31.

——, " The Phoenician Inscriptions of the Tenth Century B.C. from Byblus ", *JAOS* 67 (1947) 153-160.

——, " A Catalogue of Early Hebrew Lyric Poems (Psalm 68) ", *HUCA* 23 (1950-1951) 1-39.

——, *From the Stone Age to Christianity* (Garden City, N. Y. 2nd edition 1957).

——, " Specimens of Late Ugaritic Prose ", *BASOR* 150 (1958) 36-38.

——, " Archaic Survivals in the text of Canticles ", in *Hebrew and Semitic Studies : Presented to Godfrey Rolles Driver in celebration of his seventieth birthday 20 Aug. 1962*, edited by D. Winton Thomas and W. D. McHardy (Oxford 1963) pp. 1-7.

——, *The Proto-Sinaitic Inscriptions and their Decipherment* (Harvard Theological Studies XXII ; Cambridge, Mass. 1966).

——, *Yahweh and the Gods of Canaan* (Garden City, N. Y. 1968).

Allegro J. M., with the collaboration of A. A. Anderson, *Discoveries in the Judaean Desert, V, Qumran Cave 4. I* (*4Q158 – 4Q186*) (Oxford 1968).

Allis O. T., " Nahum, Nineveh, Elkosh ", *Evangelical Quarterly* 27 (1955) 67-80.

Alonso Schökel L., " Nota estílistica sobre la Partícula *hinnēh* ", *Biblica* 37 (1956) 74-80.

——, *Estudios de Poëtica Hebrea* (Barcelona 1963).

Alt A., " Zu den Schlussformeln der punischen Weihinschriften ", *ZAW* 60 (1944) 156-159.

Aquilina J., " Maltese as a Mixed Language ", *JSS* 3 (1958) 58-79.

Arnold W. R., " The Composition of Nahum 1 – 2 : 3 ", *ZAW* 21 (1901) 225-265.

Astour M. C., " Un texte d'Ugarit récemment découvert et ses rapports avec l'origine des cultes bachiques ", *RHR* 164 (1963) 1-15.

——, " Some New Divine Names from Ugarit ", *JAOS* 86 (1966) 277-288.

Avigad N., " Two Newly Found Hebrew Seals ", *IEJ* 13 (1963) 322-324.

——, " A Hebrew Seal with a Family Emblem ", *IEJ* 16 (1966) 50-52.

——, " Ammonite and Moabite Seals ", in *Near Eastern Archaeology in the Twentieth Century : Essays in Honor of Nelson Glueck*, edited by J. A. Sanders (Garden City, N. Y. 1970) pp. 284-292.

Barr J., *Comparative Philology and the Text of the Old Testament* (Oxford 1968).

Barthélemy D., " Redécouverte d'un chaînon manquant de l'histoire de la Septante ", *RB* 60 (1953) 18-29.

——, *Les Devanciers d'Aquila : Première publication intégrale du texte des fragments du dodécaprophéton* (VTS 10 ; Leiden 1963).

Bauer H., and Leander P., *Historische Grammatik der hebräischen Sprache* (Halle 1922).

Baumgartner W., with B. Hartmann and E. Y. Kutscher, *Hebräisches und aramäisches Lexikon zum Alten Testament* (Lieferung I, *aleph-ṭebaḥ*, Leiden 1967).

Beer, G., and Meyer, R., *Hebräische Grammatik*, I-II (Berlin 1952-1955).

Benoit P., Milik J. T. and de Vaux R., *Les Grottes de Murabbaʿât : Discoveries in the Judaean Desert*, II (Oxford 1961).

Berger P. R., " Zur Bedeutung des in den akkadischen Texten aus Ugarit bezeugten Ortsnamens Ḫīlu (Ḫl) ", *Ugarit-Forschungen* 2 (1970) 340-346.

Beyerlin W., *Origins and History of the Oldest Sinaitic Traditions* (Oxford 1965).

Bickell G., " Die hebräische Metrik ", *ZDMG* 34 (1880) 557-563.

——, *Carmina Veteris Testamenti Metrice* (Innsbruck 1882).

——, *Beiträge zur hebräische Metrik I : Das alphabetische Lied in Nahum 1,2 – 2,3* (Sitzungsberichte des phil.-hist. Classe der kaiserlichen Akademie der Wissenschaften, V ; Vienna 1894).

Birot M., *Textes administratifs de la salle 5 du palais :* (ARM IX ; Paris 1960).

Blau J., " Etymologische Untersuchungen auf Grund des palästinischen Arabisch ", *VT* 5 (1955) 337-344.

——, " Some Difficulties in the Reconstruction of ' Proto-Hebrew ' and ' Proto-Canaanite '," in *In Memoriam Paul Kahle*, edited by M. Black and G. Fohrer (BZAW 103 ; Berlin 1968) pp. 29-43.

——, and Greenfield, J. C., " Ugaritic Glosses ", *BASOR* 200 (1970) 11-17.

de Boer P. A. H., " An Inquiry into the meaning of the term *maśśā* ", *Oudtestamentische Studiën*, V (Leiden 1948) pp. 197-214.

Borger R., *Babylonisch-assyrische Lesestücke*, I-III (Rome 1963).

Bright J., *Jeremiah* (The Anchor Bible ; Garden City, N. Y. 1965).

Brockelmann C., *Grundriss der vergleichenden Grammatik der semitischen Sprachen* (Berlin 1908-1913).

Brown F., Driver S. R., and Briggs C. A., *A Hebrew and English Lexicon of the Old Testament* (Oxford 1959).

Brunner H., " Ein assyrisches Relief mit einer ägyptischen Festung (cf. Nah. 3,8ss) ", *AfO* 16 (1952) 253-262.

Buttenweiser M., *The Psalms Chronologically Treated with a New Translation* (Chicago 1938).

Carmignac J., *Les Textes de Qumran*, II (Paris 1963).

Cassuto U., " La patria del profeta Nahum ", *Giornale della Società asiatica italiana* 26 (1915) 291-302.

Cathcart K. J., " Notes on Micah 5,4-5 ", *Biblica* 49 (1968) 511-514.

——, " *Trkb qmḥ* in the Arad Ostracon and Biblical Hebrew *rekeb* ' upper millstone '", *VT* 19 (1969) 121-123.

——, " Proverbs 30,4 and Ugaritic *ḫpn* ' garment ' ", *CBQ* 32 (1970) 418-420.

Cazelles H., " La Titulaire du Roi David ", in *Mélanges bibliques rédigés en l'honneur de André Robert* (Paris 1957) pp. 131-136.

Clements R. E., " Baal-Berith of Shechem ", *JSS* 13 (1968) 21-32.

Cooke G. A., *A Textbook of North-Semitic Inscriptions* (Oxford 1903).

Cowley A., *Aramaic Papyri of the Fifth Century B.C.* (Oxford 1923).

Cross F. M., and Freedman D. N., *Early Hebrew Orthography : A Study of the Epigraphic Evidence* (American Oriental Series 36 ; New Haven 1952).

——, and Freedman D. N., " A Royal Song of Thanksgiving : II Sam. 22 = Ps 18 ", *JBL* 72 (1953) 15-34.

——, and Freedman D. N., " The Song of Miriam ", *JNES* 14 (1955) 237-250.

——, " The History of the Biblical Text in the Light of Discoveries in the Judaean Desert ", *HTR* 57 (1964) 281-299.

——, " The Contribution of the Qumran Discoveries to the Study of the Biblical text ", *IEJ* 16 (1966) 81-95.

——, " The Cave Inscriptions from Khirbet Beit Lei ", in *Near Eastern Archaeology in the Twentieth Century : Essays in Honor of Nelson Glueck*, edited by J. A. Sanders (Garden City, N. Y. 1970) pp. 299-306.

——, and Saley R. J., " Phoenician Incantations on a Plaque of the Seventh Century B. C. from Arslan Tash in Upper Syria ", *BASOR* 197 (1970) 42-49.

Culley R. C., " Metrical Analysis of Classical Hebrew Poetry ", in *Essays on the Ancient Semitic World*, edited by J. W. Wevers and D. B. Redford (Toronto 1970) pp. 12-28.

Dahood M., " Canaanite-Phoenician Influence in Qoheleth ", *Biblica* 33 (1952) 30-52 ; 191-221.

——, Review of T. H. Robinson, F. Horst, *Die Zwölf kleinen Propheten*, *CBQ* 17 (1955) 103-104.

——, " Some Northwest Semitic Words in Job ", *Biblica* 38 (1957) 306-320.

——, " The Value of Ugaritic for Textual Criticism ", *Biblica* 40 (1959) 160-170.

——, " *MKRTYHM* in Genesis 49,5 ", *CBQ* 23 (1961) 54-56.

——, " Northwest Semitic Philology and Job ", in *The Bible in Current Catholic Thought*, edited by J. L. McKenzie (New York 1962), pp. 55-74.

——, Hebrew–Ugaritic Lexicography I ", *Biblica* 44 (1963) 289-303.

——, Review of G. Garbini, *Il Semitico di Nord-Ovest*, *Orientalia* 32 (1963) 498-500.

——, *Proverbs and Northwest Semitic Philology* (Scripta Pontificii Instituti Biblici 113 ; Rome 1963).

——, Review of G. Gerleman, *Das Hohelied*, *Biblica* 45 (1964) 287-288.

——, " Hebrew–Ugaritic Lexicography II ", *Biblica* 45 (1964) 393-412.

——, " Ugaritic Lexicography " in *Mélanges Eugène Tisserant*, I (Vatican City 1964), pp. 81-104.

——, " Canaanite Words in Qoheleth 10,20 ", *Biblica* 46 (1965) 210-212.

——, Review of H. Donner and W. Röllig, *Kanaanäische und aramäische Inschriften*, *Orientalia* 34 (1965) 84-87.

——, *Ugaritic–Hebrew Philology* (Biblica et Orientalia 17 ; Rome 1965).

——, " The Phoenician Background of Qoheleth ", *Biblica* 47 (1966) 264-282.

——, " Hebrew–Ugaritic Lexicography IV ", *Biblica* 47 (1966) 403-419.

——, *Psalms I* (The Anchor Bible ; Garden City, N. Y. 1966).

——, " *SʿRT* ' storm ' in Job 4,15 ", *Biblica* 48 (1967) 544-545.

——, " A New Metrical Pattern in Biblical Poetry ", *CBQ* 29 (1967) 574-579.

——, *Psalms II* (The Anchor Bible ; Garden City, N. Y. 1968).

——, " The Psalms in Translation ", *Commentary* (September 1968) 18-26.

——, " Comparative Philology Yesterday and Today ", A Review of J. Barr, *Comparative Philology and the Text of the Old Testament*, *Biblica* 50 (1969) 70-79.

——, Review of J. M. Allegro, with the collaboration of A. A. Anderson, *Discoveries in the Judaean Desert of Jordan, V, Qumran Cave 4. I (4Q158 – 4Q186)*, *Biblica* 50 (1969) 270-272.

——, " Hebrew–Ugaritic Lexicography VII ", *Biblica* 50 (1969) 337-356.

——, " Ugaritic–Hebrew Syntax and Style ", *Ugarit-Forschungen*, I (1969) 15-36.

——, *Psalms III* (The Anchor Bible ; Garden City, N. Y. 1970).

——, " The Independent Personal Pronoun in the Oblique Case in Hebrew ", *CBQ* 32 (1970) 86-90.

——, " Hebrew–Ugaritic Lexicography VIII ", *Biblica* 51 (1970) 391-404.

Delcor M., " Nahum ", in L. Pirot and A. Clamer, *La Sainte Bible*, VIII/I (*Les Petits Prophètes* by A. Deissler and M. Delcor) (Paris 1964) pp. 361-387.

——, " Jahweh et Dagon ", *VT* 14 (1964) 136-154.

Delitzsch F., *Biblischer Kommentar über die Psalmen* (Leipzig 3rd edition 1873 ; 5th edition 1894).

——, *Das Buch Hiob* (Leipzig 1902).

Demsky A., " The Genealogy of Gibeon (I Chronicles 9 : 35-44) : Biblical and Epigraphic Considerations ", *BASOR* 202 (1971) 16-23.

Dhorme É., (ed.) *La Bible de la Pléiade* (Paris 1959).

Dietrich M., and Loretz O., " Zur ugaritischen Lexikographie (III) ", *BO* 25 (1968) 100-101.

van Dijk H. J., *Ezechiel's Prophecy on Tyre (Ez. 26,1 – 28,19) : A New Approach* (Biblica et Orientalia 20 ; Rome 1968).

van Dijk J., " Une insurrection générale au Pays de Larša avant l'avènement de Nūr-Adad ", *JCS* 19 (1965) 1-25.

Donner H., and Röllig W., *Kanaanäische und aramäische Inschriften*, 3 vols. (Wiesbaden 1962-1964).
Driver G. R., " Studies in the Vocabulary of the Old Testament III ", *JTS* 32 (1931) 361-366.
——, " Studies in the Vocabulary of the Old Testament VIII ", *JTS* 36 (1935) 293-301.
——, *Problems of the Hebrew Verbal System* (Edinburgh 1936).
——, " Linguistic and Textual Problems. Minor Prophets. II ", *JTS* 39 (1938) 260-273.
——, " Hebrew Notes on Prophets and Proverbs ", *JTS* 41 (1940) 162-175.
——, " L'interprétation du Texte massorétique à la lumière de la lexicographie hébraïque ", *ETL* 26 (1950) 337-353.
——, " Hebrew Poetic Diction ", in *Congress Volume : Copenhagen 1953* (VTS 1 ; Leiden 1953) pp. 26-39.
——, " Problems and Solutions ", *VT* 4 (1954) 225-245.
——, and Miles J. C., *The Babylonian Laws*, II (Oxford 1955).
——, *Canaanite Myths and Legends* (Edinburgh 1956).
——, *Aramaic Documents of the Fifth Century B. C.*, (abridged and revised edition ; Oxford 1957).
——, " Farewell to Queen Huzzab ", *JTS* 15 (1964) 296-298.
——, " Hebrew Homonyms ", in *Hebräische Wortforschung : Festschrift zum 80. Geburtstag von Walter Baumgartner* (VTS 16 ; Leiden 1967) pp. 50-64.
Dupont–Sommer A., " Le Commentaire de Nahum découvert près de la Mer Morte (4 QpNah) : Traduction et Notes ", *Semitica* 13 (1963) 55-88.
Dussaud R., " Le Mythe de Baʿal et d'Aliyan d'après des documents nouveaux ", *RHR* 3 (1935) 5-65.
Ehrlich A. B., *Randglossen zur hebräischen Bibel*, V (Leipzig 1912 ; reprinted Hildesheim 1968).
Eissfeldt O., *The Old Testament : An Introduction* (Oxford 1965).
Elliger K., *Das Buch der zwölf kleinen Propheten*, II (ATD 25 ; Göttingen 3rd edition 1955 ; 4th edition 1959).
Falkenstein A., and von Soden W., *Sumerische und akkadische Hymnen und Gebete* (Stuttgart 1953).
Fisher L. R., and Knutson F. B., " An Enthronement Ritual at Ugarit ", *JNES* 28 (1969) 157-167.
Fitzmyer J. A., " l^e as a Preposition and a Particle in Micah 5,1 ", *CBQ* 18 (1956) 10-13.
——, " The Aramaic Inscriptions of Sefîre I and II ", *JAOS* 81 (1961) 178-222.
——, " The Bar Cochba Period ", in *The Bible in Current Catholic Thought*, edited by J. L. McKenzie (New York 1962) pp. 133-168.
——, " The Aramaic Letter of King Adon to the Egyptian Pharaoh ", *Biblica* 46 (1965) 41-55.
——, *The Aramaic Inscriptions of Sefîre* (Biblica et Orientalia 19 ; Rome 1967).
Fleisch H., *Traité de Philologie Arabe.* Vol. I ; Préliminaire, Phonétique, Morphologie nominale (Beirut 1961).
Freedman D. N., " Isaiah 42,13 ", *CBQ* 30 (1968) 225-226.

Friedrich J., *Phönizisch–Punische Grammatik* (Analecta Orientalia 46 ; Rome 1970).
Gadd C. J., *The Fall of Nineveh* (London 1923).
Gaster T. H., " Notes on the Minor Prophets ", *JTS* 38 (1937) 163-165.
——, " Two Notes on Nahum ", *JBL* 63 (1944) 51-52.
——, *Thespis : Ritual, Myth, and Drama in the Ancient Near East* (Revised edition, New York 1966).
——, *Myth, Legend, and Custom in the Old Testament* (New York 1969).
George A., *Michée, Sophonie, Nahum : La Sainte Bible* (2nd edition, Paris 1958)
——, " Nahum ", in *Dictionnaire de la Bible : Supplément*, VI (Paris 1960) Cols. 291-301.
Gesenius W., and Buhl F., *Hebräisches und aramäisches Handwörterbuch über das Alte Testament* (Leipzig 17th edition 1915).
——, and Kautzsch E., *Gesenius' Hebrew Grammar*, translated by A. E. Cowley (Oxford 1910).
Gevirtz S., " West-Semitic Curses and the Problem of the Origins of Hebrew Law ", *VT* 11 (1961) 137-158.
Ginsberg H. L., " A Ugaritic Parallel to 2 Sam. 1,21 ", *JBL* 57 (1938) 209-213.
——, *The Legend of King Keret*, (*BASOR* Supplementary Studies Nos. 2-3 ; New Haven 1946).
Giveon R., " Two New Hebrew Seals and their Iconographic Background ", *PEQ* 93 (1961) 38-42.
Gordis R., " Psalm 9 – 10, A Textual and Exegetical Study ", *JQR* 48 (1957-1958) 104-122.
Gordon C. H., *Ugaritic Textbook.* Grammar, Texts in Transliteration, Cuneiform Selections, Glossary, Indices (Analecta Orientalia 38 ; Rome 1965).
——, *Supplement to the Ugaritic Textbook* (Rome 1967).
Gray J., " The Hebrew Concept of the Kingship of God : its origin and development ", *VT* 6 (1956) 268-285.
——, " The Kingship of God in the Prophets and Psalms ", *VT* 11 (1961) 1-29.
Gröndahl F., *Die Personennamen der Texte aus Ugarit* (Rome 1967).
Guillaume A., *Hebrew and Arabic Lexicography : A Comparative Study* (Leiden 1965 ; reprinted from *Abr-Nahrain* I-IV, 1959-1965).
Gunkel H., " Nahum 1 ", *ZAW* 13 (1893) 223-244.
——, *Schöpfung und Chaos* (Göttingen 1895).
Haldar A., *Studies in the Book of Nahum* (Uppsala 1947).
Halévy J., " Le Livre de Nahum ", *Revue sémitique d'épigraphie et d'histoire* 13 (1905) 97-123.
Hanson R. S., *The Psalms in Modern Speech* (Philadelphia 1968).
Happel J., *Der Psalm Nahum* (Nahum I) (Würzburg 1900).
——, *Das Buch des Propheten Nahum* (Würzburg 1902).
Harris Z., *Development of the Canaanite Dialects* (American Oriental Series 16 ; New Haven 1939).
Held M., " A Faithful Lover in an Old Babylonian Dialogue ", *JCS* 15 (1961) 1-26.

——, " The Action–Result (Factitive – Passive) Sequence of Identical Verbs in Biblical Hebrew and Ugaritic ", *JBL* 84 (1965) 271-282.

——, " Rhetorical Questions in Ugaritic and Biblical Hebrew ", *Eretz Israel* 9 (1969) 71-79.

——, " Studies in Biblical Homonyms in the Light of Akkadian ", *ANES* 3 (1971) 46-55.

Hillers, D. R., *Treaty-Curses and the Old Testament Prophets* (Biblica et Orientalia 16 ; Rome 1964).

——, " A Convention in Hebrew Literature : The Reaction to Bad News " *ZAW* 77 (1965) 86-89.

Himmelfarb M., " Translating the Psalms ", *Commentary* 45 (February 1968) 72-76.

——, " The Psalms in Translation ", *Commentary* 46 (September 1968) 26-38.

Hoffner H. A., " Composite Nouns, Verbs and Adjectives in Hittite ", *Orientalia* 35 (1966) 377-402.

Holman J., " Analysis of the Text of Ps. 139 " ; *BZ* 14 (1970) 37-71.

van Hoonacker A., *Les Douze Petits Prophètes* (Paris 1908).

Horst F., *Die zwölf kleinen Propheten : Nahum bis Maleachi*, (HAT ; Tübingen 1938, 2nd edition 1954).

Huesman J., " Finite Uses of the Infinitive Absolute ", *Biblica* 37 (1956) 271-295.

——, " The Infinitive Absolute and the Waw + Perfect Problem ", *Biblica* 37 (1956) 410-434.

Humbert P., " Nahoum 2,9 " *RÉJ* 83 (1927) 74-76.

——, " La Vision de Nahoum 2,4-11 ", *AfO* 5 (1928-9) 14-19.

——, " En Marge du dictionnaire hebraïque ", *ZAW* 62 (1949-1950) 199-207.

Hummel H. D., " Enclitic *Mem* in Early Northwest Semitic, especially Hebrew ", *JBL* 76 (1957) 85-107.

Hyatt J. P., " Nahum ", in *Peake's Commentary on the Bible* (London 1962) pp. 635-636.

Jacobsen T., and Lloyd S., *Sennacherib's Aqueduct at Jerwan* (The University of Chicago Oriental Institute Publications 24 ; Chicago 1935).

Jean C. F. and Hoftijzer J., *Dictionnaire des inscriptions sémitiques de l'Ouest* (Leiden 1965).

Jeremias Jörg, *Kultprophetie und Gerichtsverkündigung in der späten Königszeit Israels* (Neukirchen-Vluyn 1970).

Jirku A., " Eine Renaissance des Hebräischen ", *FuF* 32 (1958) 211-212.

Johnson A. R., *Sacral Kingship in Ancient Israel* (Cardiff 1955).

——, *The Cultic Prophet in Ancient Israel* (Revised edition, Cardiff 1962).

Joüon P., *Grammaire de l'hébreu biblique* (Rome 1923).

Junker H., *Die zwölf kleinen Propheten*, II (HSAT VIII ; Bonn 1938).

——, " Unité, Composition et Genre Littéraire des Psaumes IX et X ", *RB* 60 (1953) 161-169.

Kissane E., *The Book of Isaiah*, I (Dublin 1941).

Knudtzon J. A., *Die El-Amarna Tafeln* (Leipzig 1907).

Köhler L., and Baumgartner W., *Lexicon in Veteris Testamenti Libros* (Leiden 1953).

——, *Supplementum ad Lexicon in Veteris Testamenti Libros*, (Leiden 1958).

Kraeling E. M., *Commentary on the Prophets*, II (Camden, N. J. 1966). (*The Book of Nahum*, pp. 229-241).

Kramer S. N., *History Begins at Sumer* (Garden City, N. Y. 1959).

Kutscher E. Y., " Contemporary Studies in Northwestern Semitic ", *JSS* 10 (1965) 21-51.

Lambdin T. O., " Egyptian Words in Tell El Amarna Letter No. 14 ", *Orientalia* 22 (1953) 362-369.

——, " Put ", *IDB*, Vol. 3, p. 971.

Lambert W. G., *Babylonian Wisdom Literature* (Oxford 1960).

——, and Millard A. R., *Atra-Ḫasīs : the Babylonian Story of the Flood* (Oxford 1969).

Landsberger B., *The Fauna of Ancient Mesopotamia.* Materialen zum sumerischen Lexicon VIII/I : Tablet XIII (Rome 1961).

——, *The Fauna of Ancient Mesopotamia.* Materialen zum sumerischen Lexicon VIII/2 : Tablets XIV and XVIII (Rome 1962).

Lane E. W., *Arabic-English Lexicon*, 8 vols. (London 1863-1893).

Leonardi G., " Note su alcuni versetti del Salmo 104 ", *Biblica* 49 (1968) 238-242.

Leslau W., " Southeast Semitic Cognates to the Akkadian Vocabulary. III ", *JAOS* 89 (1969) 10-22.

Lidzbarski M., *Handbuch der nordsemitischen Epigraphik* (Weimar 1898).

——, *Ephemeris für semitische Epigraphik*, I (Giessen 1902).

Lifshitz B., " The Greek Documents from the Cave of Horror ", *IEJ* 12 (1962) 201-207.

Lindblom J., " Lot-casting in the Old Testament ", *VT* 12 (1962) 164-178.

Lipinski E., " Nimrod et Assur ", *RB* 73 (1966) 77-93.

Loewenstamm S. E., " The Lord is my strength and my glory ", *VT* 19 (1969) 464-470.

Loretz O., " Neues Verständnis einiger Schriftstellen mit Hilfe des Ugaritichen," *BZ* 2 (1968) 287-291.

McCarthy D. J., " Vox *bśr* praeparat vocem ' evangelium '", *Verbum Domini* 42 (1964) 26-33.

McDaniel T. F., " Philological Studies in Lamentations I ", *Biblica* 49 (1968) 27-53.

——, " Philological Studies in Lamentations II ", *Biblica* 49 (1968) 199-220.

——, " The Alleged Sumerian Influence upon Lamentations ", *VT* 18 (1968) 198-209.

McKenzie J. L., *Second Isaiah* (The Anchor Bible ; Garden City, N. Y. 1968).

Maier W., *The Book of Nahum : A Commentary* (St. Louis 1959).

Marti K., *Das Dodekapropheton* (KHC ; Tübingen 1904).

Martin M., " The Use of Second Person Singular Suffixes in IQIs ", *Muséon* 70 (1957) 127-144.

May H. G., " Some Cosmic Connotations of *Mayim Rabbim* ", *JBL* 74 (1955) 9-21.

Meyer R., *Review of Hebrew and Semitic Studies. Presented to Godfrey Rolles Driver in celebration of his seventieth birthday 20 Aug. 1962* edited by D. Winton Thomas and W. D. McHardy, *OLZ* 62 (1967) Col. 371.

Michaud H., Review of J. B. Pritchard, *Hebrew Inscriptions and Stamps from Gibeon*, *VT* 10 (1960) 102-106.

Migne J. P., (ed.) *Patrologiae cursus completus : Series Latina* 221 Tomes (Paris 1844 ff.).

——, *Patrologiae cursus completus : Series Graeca* 161 Tomes (Paris 1857 ff.).

Miller P. D., " El the Warrior ", *HTR* 60 (1967) 411-431.

——, " Ugaritic ǦZR and Hebrew ʿZR II ", *Ugarit-Forschungen* 2 (1970) 159-175.

——, " Animal Names as Designations in Ugaritic and Hebrew ", *Ugarit-Forschungen* 2 (1970) 177-186.

de Moor J. C., " Der *mdl* Baals im Ugaritischen ", *ZAW* 78 (1966) 69-71.

——, " Studies in the New Alphabetic Texts from Ras Shamra I ", *Ugarit-Forschungen* I (1969) 167-188.

——, " Studies in the New Alphabetic Texts from Ras Shamra II ", *Ugarit-Forschungen* 2 (1970) 303-327.

Moran W. L., " The Use of the Canaanite Infinitive Absolute as a Finite Verb in the Amarna Letters from Byblos ", *JCS* 4 (1950) 169-172.

——, " New Evidence on Canaanite *taqtulū*(*na*) " *JCS* 5 (1951) 33-35.

——, " Amarna *šumma* in Main Clauses ", *JCS* 7 (1953) 78-80.

——, " The Hebrew Language in its Northwest Semitic Background ", in *The Bible and the Ancient Near East, Essays in honor of William Foxwell Albright*, edited by G. E. Wright (Garden City, N. Y. 1961) pp. 54-72.

——, " Some Remarks on the Song of Moses ", *Biblica* 43 (1962) 317-327.

——, " **taqtul* - Third Masculine Singular ? ", *Biblica* 45 (1964) 80-82.

——, " New Evidence from Mari on the History of Prophecy ", *Biblica* 50 (1969) 15-56.

Moscati S., *An Introduction to the Comparative Grammar of the Semitic Languages* (Wiesbaden 1964).

Mowinckel S., " Drive and/or Ride in the O. T.", *VT* 12 (1962) 277-299.

Muilenburg J., " Hebrew Rhetoric : Repetition and Style " in *Congress Volume : Copenhagen 1953* (VTS 1 ; Leiden 1953) pp. 97-111.

——, " Form Criticism and Beyond ", *JBL* 88 (1969) 1-18.

Murphy R. T. A., " Nahum ", in *The Jerome Biblical Commentary* edited by R. E. Brown, J. A. Fitzmyer, R. E. Murphy (Englewood Cliffs, N. J. 1968) pp. 293-295.

Myers J. M., *Ezra. Nehemiah* (The Anchor Bible ; Garden City, N. Y. 1965).

Nestle G., " Where is the birthplace of the Prophet Nahum to be sought ? ", *PEQ* (1879) 136-138.

Noth M., *Die israelitischen Personennamen im Rahmen der gemeinsemitischen Namengebung* (Stuttgart 1928 ; reprinted Hildesheim 1966).

——, *Das System der zwölf Stämme Israels* (Stuttgart 1930 ; reprinted Darmstadt 1966).

Nötscher F., *Zwölfprophetenbuch oder kleine Propheten* (Echter-Bibel ; Würzburg 1948).

Nowack W., *Die kleinen Propheten* (HKAT III ; Göttingen 1897 ; 2nd edition 1904 ; 3rd edition 1922).

O'Callaghan R. T., " Echoes of Canaanite Literature in the Psalms ", *VT* 4 (1954) 164-176.

O'Cellaigh G. C., " And *So* David did to *all the cities* of Ammon ", *VT* 12 (1962) 179-189.

Oppenheim A. L., and Hartman L. F., " The Domestic Animals of Ancient Mesopotamia, according to the XIIIth tablet of the series *ḪAR.ra=ḫubullû** ", *JNES* 4 (1945) 152-177.

——, " The Archives of the Palace of Mari II : A Review Article ", *JNES* 13 (1954) 141-148.

——, *et al.*, *The Assyrian Dictionary* of the Oriental Institute of the University of Chicato (Chicago 1956 ff.).

Parrot A., *Nineveh and the Old Testament* (New York 1955).

van der Ploeg J., " Les chefs du peuple Israël et leur titres ", *RB* 57 (1950) 40-61.

Pope M., *El in the Ugaritic Texts* (VTS 2 ; Leiden 1955).

——, *Job* (The Anchor Bible ; Garden City, N. Y. 1965).

——, " Marginalia to M. Dahood's *Ugaritic–Hebrew Philology* ", JBL 85 (1966) 455-466.

——, " A Mare in Pharaoh's Chariotry ", *BASOR* 200 (1970) 56-61.

Pritchard J. B., ed., *Ancient Near Eastern Texts* (2nd edition, Princeton 1955).

——, *Hebrew Inscriptions and Stamps from Gibeon* (Philadelphia 1959).

——, *The Ancient Near East: Supplement* (Princeton 1969).

Rabin C., " Hittite Words in Hebrew ", *Orientalia* 32 (1963) 113-139.

Rankin O. S., " Alliteration in Hebrew Poetry " ; Review Article of I. Gábor, *Der Hebräische Urrhythmus* (BZAW 52 ; Giessen 1929), *JTS* 31 (1930) 285-291.

Reider J., " A New Ishtar Epithet in the Bible ", *JNES* 8 (1949) 104-107.

Rinaldi G., " Alcuni Termini Ebraici relativi alla Letteratura ", *Biblica* 40 (1959) 267-289.

Ringgren H., *Israelite Religion* (Philadelphia 1966).

Robinson T. H. and Horst F., *Die zwölf kleinen Propheten* (HAT ; Tübingen 1938, 2nd edition 1954).

Rössler O., " Die Präfixkonjugation qal der Verba 1ae Nun im Althebräischen und das Problem der sogenannten Tempora ", *ZAW* 74 (1962) 125-141.

Rowley H. H., Review of A. Haldar, *Studies in the Book of Nahum*, *BO* 4 (1947) 60-61.

Ryckmans G., " Notes Épigraphiques : Cinquième Série VIII — Le sens de quelques termes usites comme titres de stèles ", *Muséon* 71 (1958) 125-139.

——, Review of A. Dupont-Sommer and L. Robert, *La déesse de Hiéropolis Castabala* (*Cilicie*) (Paris 1964), *Muséon* 78 (1965) 467-469.

Saggs H. W. F., " Nahum and the Fall of Nineveh ", *JTS* 20 (1969) 220-225.

Sarna N. M., " The Interchange of the Prepositions *Beth* and *Min* in Biblical Hebrew ", *JBL* 78 (1959) 310-316.

——, " Ezekiel 8 : 17 : A Fresh Examination ", *HTR* 57 (1964) 347-352.

Saydon P. P., " Assonance in Hebrew as a Means of Expressing Emphasis ", *Biblica* 36 (1955) 36-50 ; 287-304.

Schaeffer C. F. A., " Ausgrabungen und Forschungreisen ; neue Entdeckungen in Ugarit ", *AfO* 19 (1959-60) 193-195.

——, (ed.) *Ugaritica V* (Mission de Ras Shamra XVI ; Paris 1968).
Schiemann R., " Covenanting with the Princes ; Neh VI 2 ", *VT* 17 (1967) 367-369.
Schmidt W. H., *Königtum Gottes in Ugarit und Israel* (Berlin 1961).
Scott R. B. Y., *Proverbs. Ecclesiastes* (The Anchor Bible ; Garden City, N. Y. 1965).
Sellin E., *Das Zwölfprophetenbuch :* Nahum – Maleachi (KAT ; Leipzig 2nd and 3rd editions 1929-1930).
Serra R., Algunos posibles ejemplos de interferencias de preposiciones en el hebreo biblico ", *Claretianum* 7 (1967) 293-317.
Skehan P. W., " The Scrolls and the Old Testament Text ", in *New Directions in Biblical Archaeology*, edited by D. N. Freedman and J. C. Greenfield (Garden City, N. Y. 1971) 99-112.
Smith J. M. P., *A Critical and Exegetical Commentary on the Books of Micah, Zephaniah, and Nahum* (ICC ; Edinburgh 1912).
von Soden W., *Akkadisches Handwörterbuch* (Wiesbaden 1959 ff.).
——, " Kleine Beiträge zum Ugaritischen ", in *Hebräische Wortforschung : Festschrift zum 80. Geburtstag von Walter Baumgartner* (VTS 16 ; Leiden 1967) pp. 291-300.
Soggin J. A., " La ' negazione ' in Geremia 4, 27 e 5, 10a, cfr. 5, 18b ", *Biblica* 46 (1965) 56-59.
Speiser E. A., " The Biblical *Nāśî'* ", *CBQ* 25 (1963) 111-117.
——, *Genesis* (The Anchor Bible ; Garden City, N. Y. 1964).
Sperber A., " Biblical Exegesis ", *JBL* 64 (1945) 39-140.
——, *A Historical Grammar of Biblical Hebrew* (Leiden 1966).
Stadelmann L. I. J., *The Hebrew Conception of the World* (Analecta Biblica 39 ; Rome 1970).
Stamm J. J., *Die akkadische Namengebung* (Leipzig 1939).
Stonehouse G. G. V., *The Books of the Prophets. Zephaniah and Nahum* (Westminster Commentaries ; London 1929).
Strugnell J., " Notes en marge du volume V des ' Discoveries in the Judaean Desert of Jordan ' ", *Revue de Qumran* No. 26 (1970) 163-276.
Taylor C. L., " Nahum : Introduction and Exegesis ", *The Interpreter's Bible*, VI (New York 1959) pp. 953-969.
Thomas D. Winton, " The Root *mkr* in Hebrew ", *JTS* 37 (1936) 388-389.
——, " The Language of the Old Testament ", in *Record and Revelation* edited by H. W. Robinson (Oxford 1938) pp. 374-402.
——, Review of A. Haldar, *Studies in the Book of Nahum*, *JJS* 1 (1948) 122-124.
——, " A Further Note on the Root *mkr* in Hebrew ", *JTS* 3 (1952) 314.
——, (ed.) *Documents from Old Testament Times* (London 1958).
——, " bᵉliyya'al in the Old Testament ", in *Biblical and Patristic Studies in Memory of Robert Pierce Casey*, edited by J. Neville Birdsall and R. W. Thomson (Freiburg 1963) pp. 11-19.
——, *The Text of the Revised Psalter* (London 1963).
Torczyner H., " Presidential Address ", *JPOS* 16 (1936) 1-8.
Tournay R., " Recherche sur la chronologie des Psaumes ", *RB* 65 (1958) 321-357.

——, Review of J. H. Eaton, *Obadiah, Nahum, Habakkuk, Zephaniah* (London 1961), *RB* 69 (1962) 304.

——, Review of A. Deissler and M. Delcor, *Les Petits Prophètes* (Paris 1964), *RB* 72 (1965) 427-429.

Tromp N., *Primitive Conceptions of Death and the Netherworld in the Old Testament* (Biblica et Orientalia 21 ; Rome 1969).

Ullendorff E., " The Contribution of South Semitics to Hebrew Lexicography ", *VT* 6 (1956) 190-198.

——, " Ugaritic Marginalia II ", *JSS* 7 (1962) 339-351.

de Vaux R., *Ancient Israel : Its Life and Institutions* (London 1961).

de Vries S. J., " The Acrostic of Nahum in the Jerusalem Liturgy ", *VT* 16 (1966) 476-481.

Wagner M., *Die lexikalischen und grammatikalischen Aramaismen im alttestamentlichen Hebräisch* (BZAW 96 ; Berlin 1966).

Ward W. A., " Some Egypto–Semitic Roots ", *Orientalia* 31 (1962) 397-412.

Wehr H., *A Dictionary of Modern Written Arabic*, edited by J. Milton Cowan (Wiesbaden 1960).

van der Weiden W. A., " Abstractum pro concreto ; phaenomenon stilisticum ", *Verbum Domini* 44 (1966) 43-52.

——, *Le Livre des Proverbes : Notes Philologiques* (Biblica et Orientalia 23 ; Rome 1970).

Weill J., " Nahoum, II, 9-12, et Josèphe (Ant., IX xi § 239-241) ", *REJ* 76 (1923) 96-98.

Weingreen J., " The Construct-Genitive Relation in Hebrew Syntax ", *VT* 4 (1954) 50-59.

Weiss R., " A Comparison between the Massoretic and Qumran Texts of Nahum III, 1-11 ", *Revue de Qumran* No. 15 (1963) 433-439.

Wieder A. A., " Ugaritic–Hebrew Lexicographical Notes ", *JBL* 84 (1965) 160-164.

Williams R. J., " The Passive *Qal* Theme in Hebrew ", in *Essays on the Ancient Semitic World* ", edited by J. W. Wevers and D. B. Redford (Toronto 1970) pp. 43-50.

Wilson J. A., *The Burden of Egypt : An Interpretation of Ancient Egyptian Culture* (Chicago 1951).

Wiseman D. J., *Chronicles of Chaldaean Kings (626-556 B.C.) in the British Museum* (London 1956 ; reprinted 1961).

Yadin Y., "Pesher Nahum (4Q pNah) Reconsidered", *IEJ* 21 (1971) 1-12.

Ziegler J., (ed.) *Septuaginta : Vetus Testamentum Graecum Auctoritate Academiae Litterarum Gottingensis editum : XIII Duodecim prophetae* (Göttingen 1943 ; 2nd edition 1967).

Zimmer H., *Akkadische Fremdwörter als Beweis für babylonischen Kultureinfluss* (2nd edition, Leipzig 1917).

Zorell F., *Lexicon hebraicum et aramaicum Veteris Testamenti* (Rome 1957).

Chapter I

Nahum 1:1 - 2:1

Text : Nahum 1 : 1-5a

Verse	Text	Syllable Count	Stress Count
1	מַשָּׂא נִינְוֵה סֵפֶר חֲזוֹן נַחוּם הָאֶלְקֹשִׁי		
2	אֵל קַנּוֹא וְנֹקֵם יַהְוֶה	8	4
	נֹקֵם יַהְוֶה וּבַעַל חֵמָה	9	4
	נֹקֵם יַהְוֶה לְצָרָיו	7	3
	וְנוֹטֵר הוּא לְאֹיְבָיו	8	3
3	יַהְוֶה אֶרֶךְ אַפַּיִם וּגְדָל־כֹּחַ	11	4
	וְנַקֵּה לֹא יְנַקֶּה יַהְוֶה	9	4
	בְּסוּפָה וּבִשְׂעָרָה דַּרְכּוֹ	10	3
	וְעָנָן אֲבַק רַגְלָיו	7	3
4	גּוֹעֵר בַּיָּם וַיַּבְּשֵׁהוּ	9	3
	וְכָל־הַנְּהָרוֹת הֶחֱרִיב	9	3
	אֻמְלַל בָּשָׁן וְכַרְמֶל	7	3
	וּפֶרַח לְבָנוֹן אֻמְלָל	8	3
5	הָרִים רָעֲשׁוּ מִמֶּנּוּ	8	3
	וְהַגְּבָעוֹת הִתְמֹגָגוּ	9	3

Translation : Nahum 1 : 1-5a

1 An oracle concerning Nineveh. The book of the vision of Nahum
the Elkoshite.

2 A jealous and avenging God (El) is Yahweh,
avenging is Yahweh and a Lord (Ba'al) of wrath.

Avenging is Yahweh on his foes,
and he rages against his enemies.

3 Yahweh is slow to anger but great in power,
and Yahweh will certainly not acquit (the guilty).

In the whirlwind and in the storm is his way,
and the clouds are the dust of his feet.

4 He rebukes the sea and dries it up,
and all the rivers he parches.

Bashan and Carmel wither,
and the bloom of Lebanon withers.

5 The mountains shake before him,
and the hills melt away.

Text: Nahum 1:5b-10

Syllable Count	Stress Count		
9	3		וַתִּשָּׂא הָאָרֶץ מִפָּנָיו
9	3		וְתֵבֵל וְכָל־יֹשְׁבֵי בָהּ
8	4	6	לִפְנֵי זַעְמוֹ מִי יַעֲמוֹד
9	4		וּמִי יָקוּם בַּחֲרוֹן אַפּוֹ
8	3		חֲמָתוֹ נִתְּכָה כָאֵשׁ
10	3		וְהַצֻּרִים נִתְּצוּ מִמֶּנּוּ
10	5	7	טוֹב יַהְוֶה לְמָעוֹז בְּיוֹם צָרָה
11	5		וְיֹדֵעַ חֹסֵי בוֹ בְּשֶׁטֶף עֹבֵר
9	3	8	כָּלָה יַעֲשֶׂה מִקּוֹמֵהוּ
9	3		וְאֹיְבָיו יְרַדֶּף־חֹשֶׁךְ
8	3	9	מַה־תְּחַשְּׁבוּן אֶל־יַהְוֶה
5	3		כָּלָה הוּא עֹשֶׂה
9	4		לֹא תָקוּם פַּעֲמַיִם צָרָה
7	3	10	כִּי עַד סִירִים סְבֻכִים
8	3		וּכְסָבְאָם סְבוּאִים
9	4		אֻכְּלוּ כְּקַשׁ יָבֵשׁ מָלֵא

Translation: Nahum 1:5b-10

The earth is laid waste before him,
the world and all who dwell in it.

6 Before his indignation who can stand,
and who can rise in the heat of his anger?

His wrath pours out like fire,
and the rocks are broken up before him.

7 Better is Yahweh than a fortress on the day of siege,
and he cares for those seeking refuge in him when the
flood sweeps over.

8 He will make an end of his assailants,
and his foes he will pursue into Darkness.

9 Why do you plot against Yahweh?
He is one who makes an end;
his adversaries will not rise up twice.

10 For again they are entangled thorns,
and like drunkards sodden with drink;
they will be consumed like very dry chaff.

Text : Nahum 1 : 11-14

Syllable Count	Stress Count	
6	3	11 מִמֵּךְ יָצָא חֹשֵׁב
5	2	עַל יַהְוֶה רָעָה
6	2	יֹעֵץ בְּלִיָּעַל
		12 כֹּה אָמַר יַהְוֶה
8	4	אִם שְׁלֵמִים וְכֵן רַבִּים
8	2	וְנָגֹזּוּ וְעָבְרוּ
8	4	עִנִּתִךְ לֹא אֲעַנֵּךְ עוֹד
8	3	13 וְעַתָּה אֶשְׁבֹּר מֹטֵהוּ
4	1	מֵעָלָיִךְ
9	3	וּמוֹסְרֹתַיִךְ אֲנַתֵּק
8	3	14 וְצִוָּה עָלֶיךְ יַהְוֶה
8 (9)	4	לֹא יִזָּרַע־מ שִׁמְךָ עוֹד
6	2	מִבֵּית אֱלֹהֶיךְ
8	3	אַכְרִית פֶּסֶל וּמַסֵּכָה
9	4	אָשִׂים קִבְרֶךְ כִּי קַלּוֹתָ

Translation: Nahum 1:11-14

11 From you has gone forth one who plots
evil against Yahweh,
one who is a counsellor of Belial.

12 Thus says Yahweh:
Even though they are strong and many,
they will be cut down and overwhelmed,
I have oppressed you, but I will not oppress you again.

13 And now I will break his yoke
away from you
and your bonds I will snap.

14 And Yahweh commands thus concerning you:
Your name shall not be sown again;
From your temple
I will cut off the carved and molten image(s);
I will devastate your grave because you are worthless.

Text: Nahum 2:1

Syllable Count	Stress Count		
11	4	הִנֵּה עַל הֶהָרִים רַגְלֵי מְבַשֵּׂר	1
4	2	מַשְׁמִיעַ שָׁלוֹם	
8	3	חָגִּי יְהוּדָה חַגַּיִךְ	
7	2	שַׁלְּמִי נְדָרָיִךְ	
13	5	כִּי לֹא יוֹסִיף עוֹד לַעֲבוֹר בָּךְ בְּלִיַּעַל	
4	2	כֻּלֹּה נִכְרָת :	

Translation: Nahum 2:1

1 Behold upon the mountains the feet of one who
brings good tidings,
of one who announces peace!
Celebrate your feasts, O Judah!
Fulfill your vows.
Because Belial shall not pass over you again,
he has been wholly destroyed.

Philological Commentary

1 : 1

maśśā : " An oracle ". *maśśāʾ* should be rendered " oracle " or " utterance ". Some translators follow the ancient versions and give *maśśāʾ* the meaning " burden " (1). But the verb *nāśāʾ* is used with the sense of " raising the voice, uttering ". So, for example, Is. 3 : 7, *yiśśāʾ bayyôm hahûʾ lēʾmōr*, " In that day he will speak out saying " : (*RSV*). Heb. *nāśāʾ qôl* is the equivalent of Ugar. *nšʾ g*. Hence in Is. 42 : 11, *yiś*^{e}*ʾû midbār w*^{e}*ʿărāyw*, " Let the steppe and its tamarisks raise their voices " (2), *yiś*^{e}*ʾû* need not be emended to *yāśûśû* as suggested by *BH*^{3}, since the verse ends with *mērōʾš hārîm yiṣwāḥû*, "from the tops of the mountains let them shout ". The pair *yiś*^{e}*ʾû*//*yiṣwāḥû* is matched in *UT*, 127 : 14-16, *wypqd krt ṯʿ yšu gh wyṣḥ*, " then Keret the Noble commands, raising his voice and crying " (Ginsberg, *ANET* 149). Likewise, Job 21 : 12, *yiś*^{e}*ʾû k*^{e}*tōp w*^{e}*kinnôr w*^{e}*yiśm*^{e}*ḥû l*^{e}*qôl ʿûgāb*, " They sing to the timbrel and harp, Revel to the tune of the flute " (3), need not be interfered with. (*BH*^{3} again suggests *yāśîśû* for *yiś*^{e}*ʾû*). For the pairing of *yiś*^{e}*ʾû* and *yiśm*^{e}*ḥû* matches the same collocation in *UT*, 49 : III : 14-17, *šmḫ lṭpn il dpid pʿnh lhdm yṯpd wyprq lṣb wyṣḥq yšu gh wyṣḥ*, " The Kindly One El Benign's glad. His feet on the footstool he sets, and parts his jaws and laughs. He lifts up his voice and cries " (*ANET* 140) (4). For further examples

(1) So, for example, W. Maier, *The Book of Nahum : A Commentary* (St. Louis 1959), who writes (p. 146) that the term *maśśāʾ* introduces " burden-bearing statements against oppressive sinful peoples " ! For the pun on the word *maśśāʾ* (which *can* mean " burden " in other contexts) in Jer. 23 : 33, consult J. Bright, *Jeremiah*, p. 153.

(2) Following the suggestion of M. Dahood that *ʿryw* here is a *Nebenform* of Ugaritic and Hebrew *ʿrʿr*, " tamarisk ". Cf. *Biblica* 50 (1969) 356.

(3) Translation of M. Pope, *Job*, p. 142. For a different version and interpretation of the verse, cf. M. Dahood, *Psalms III*, p. 358.

(4) Note also the other Canaanite pair *šmḫ*/*ṣḥq* here, which M. Dahood has pointed out in Eccles. 2 : 2, *liśḥôq ... ûl*^{e}*śimḥāh*. Cf. " The Phoenician Background of Qoheleth ", *Biblica* 47 (1966) 267.

of these pairs, see *UT*, 49 : I : 11 ; 49 : II : 11-12 ; 67 : II : 20-21 ; 2 Aqht : II : 9-12. *nāśā'* should be studied in the following texts : Gen. 21 : 16 ; 27 : 38 ; 29 : 11 ; Exod. 20 : 7 ; Num. 14 : 1 ; 23 : 7,18 ; 24 : 3 f ; Judg. 2 : 4 ; 9 : 7 ; 2 Kings 19 : 4 ; Is. 14 : 4 ; 24 : 14 ; 52 : 8 ; Jer 7 : 16, 29 ; 9 : 9 ; Ezek. 19 : 1 ; 26 : 17 ; 27 : 2,32 ; 28 : 12 ; 32 : 2 ; Amos 5 : 1 ; Mic. 2 : 4 ; Hab. 2 : 6 ; Ps. 15 : 3 ; 93 : 3 ; Job 27 : 1. A number of scholars have refused to accept the definition " oracle, utterance " for *maśśā'*, but its relation to *nāśa'* (*qôl*) seems unquestionable (5).

maśśā', " oracle ", occurs frequently : Is. 13 : 1 ; 14 : 28 ; 15 : 1 ; 17 : 1 ; 19 : 1 ; etc. ; Ezek. 12 : 10 ; Hab. 1 : 1 ; Zech. 9 : 1 ; Mal. 1 : 1 ; Lam. 2 : 14. In 2 Kings 9 : 25, both verb *nāśā'* and noun *maśśā'* occur together (6).

nînᵉwēh : " Nineveh ". Akk. *Ninua, Ninā* but also *Ninuwa*.

ḥᵃzôn : " vision of ". *ḥāzôn*, " vision ", is related to *ḥāzāh :* Is. 13 : 1, *maśśā' bābel 'ᵃšer ḥāzāh yᵉšaʿyāhû ben 'āmôṣ*, " The oracle concerning Babylon which Isaiah the son of Amoz saw " ; Hab. 1 : 1, *hammaśśā' 'ᵃšer ḥāzāh ḥᵃbaqqûq hannābî'*, " The oracle which Habakkuk the prophet saw " ; Lam. 2 : 14, *wayyeḥᵉzû lāk maśśā'ôt*, " but have seen for you oracles ". Note also Aram. Afis *KAI*, 202 : 12, *ḥzyn*, " seer ".

naḥûm : " Nahum ". The name occurs only here in the Old Testament, though there are other names from the same root : *nᵉḥemyāh* (Nehemiah) ; *naḥᵃmānî* (Nahamani : Neh. 7 : 7) ; *tanḥūmet* (Tanhumeth : Jer. 40 : 8) ; *mᵉnaḥēm* (Menahem : 2 Kings 15 : 14-23) ; the last-mentioned name occurs in texts from Ugarit as *mnḥm*. *naḥûm* may be a shortened form of *nḥmyh* or *nḥm'l*. There is no need to surmise that *naḥûm* was not the prophet's birth name and that it was given

(5) A strong opponent of the meaning " utterance, oracle ", is P. A. H. de Boer, *Oudtestamentische Studiën* V (Leiden 1948) pp. 197-214. Notice also the title of J. A. Wilson, *The Burden of Egypt*. Compare however G. Rinaldi, *Biblica* 40 (1959) 278, " Ma il collegamento etimologico del tutto probabile, con *nś'* (*qwl*) ' alzare la voce ', invece che a un fatto di forma o un contenuto, rinvia a un impiego del testo o a un modo particolare con cui si faceva quel-l'impiego ". De Boer's position has also been rejected by A. R. Johnson, *Cultic Prophet*, p. 41.

(6) M. Noth relates *nāśî* (usually rendered " prince ") to *nāśā' qôl* and gives it the meaning " speaker ". Cf. Noth's *Das System der zwölf Stämme Israels* pp. 151 ff. But see E. A. Speiser, *CBQ* 25 (1963) 111-117, who disagrees with Noth and renders *nāśî'* " chieftain ". Another discussion is found in J. van der Ploeg, *RB* 57 (1950) 40-61.

to him at a much later date because of the content of his message ([7]). The name is attested frequently in Northwest Semitic inscriptions. One of several ostraca from Arad (published in 1966) ([8]), which possibly dates from the 7th century B.C., is addressed to a certain *nḥm*. From Lachish comes a bulla with a Hebrew seal impression which reads : *lnḥm bn ʿnnyhw*, " Belonging to Nahum son of ʿAnanyahu "([9]).

hāʾelqōšî : " the Elkoshite ", is gentilic. Other biblical examples are Jer. 26 : 18 and Mic. 1 : 1, *mîkāh hammôraštî*, " Micah the Morashtite ", and Jer. 29 : 27, *yirmᵉyāhû hāʿannᵉtōtî*, " Jeremiah the Annothothite ". Compare Proto-Canaanite *ṯbl ʿrqy*, " Shobal the Arkite ", found in the St. Louis seal cylinder. ([10]) There are many examples in the Ras Shamra texts. One example is *UT*, 62 : 53, *ilmlk šbny*, " Elimelek the Shabnite ".

The location of Elkosh is unknown and various regions have been suggested. Jerome ([11]) proposed " Elcesi ", a village in Galilee, and Pseudo-Epiphanius ([12]) speaks of Beth-gabre of the tribe of Simeon. Beth-Gabre has been linked with modern Beit-Jibrin, about twenty miles south-west of Jerusalem. ([13]) An unlikely identification is Al-Qush, about twenty-five miles north of Modern Mosul.

1 : 2

qannôʾ : " jealous ". The form *qannôʾ* occurs only twice in the Old Testament (cf. *ʾēl qannôʾ* in Josh. 24 : 19), the more usual form being *qannāʾ* (cf. *ʾēl qannāʾ* in Exod. 20 : 5 ; 34 : 14 ; Deut. 4 : 24 ; 5 : 9 ; 6 : 15). Albright ([14]) regards *qannāʾ* as the later form, but compare J. Halévy, who describes *qannôʾ* as a " forme dialectale phénicisante ". ([15]) Gordon draws attention to Ugar. *qnum* in *UT*, 2078 :

([7]) For notions along these lines, cf. A. Haldar, *Studies*, p. 148 ; J. P. Hyatt, " Nahum ", in Peake's *Commentary on the Bible*, p. 635.

([8]) Y. Aharoni, *IEJ* 16 (1966) 1-7, esp. 4 ; also *idem*, *BASOR* 184 (1966) 14-16 ; *BA* 31 (1968) 14.

([9]) *Idem*, *IEJ* 18 (1968) 166.

([10]) W. F. Albright, *PSID* 11, No. 6.

([11]) *Commentariorum in Naum Prophetam*, PL 25, 1231.

([12]) *Liber de vitis Prophetarum. De Prophetis, eorumque obitu ac sepultura*, PG 43, 409.

([13]) For efforts to be more precise, cf. G. Nestle, *PEQ* (1879) 136-138 ; U. Cassuto, *Giornale della Società asiatica italiana* 26 (1915) 291-302.

([14]) *From the Stone Age to Christianity*, p. 309.

([15]) *Revue sémitique d'epigraphie et d'histoire* 13 (1905) 100.

1. (16) However, he observes that the shift from *â* to *ô* does not take place in standard Ugaritic and explains *ṯut*, " ewes ", in *UT*, 1153 : 3 in contrast to *ṯat* in *UT*, 49 : II : 7,29, as the infiltration of the shift from *â* to *ô* into the prose of Ugarit. (17) Dahood has added further interesting notes to the discussion, remarking that in the Ugaritic syllabary, *q* is written syllabically as *qu*. (18)

Albright may well be right when he says that the " outstanding concept of God in the Prophetic Age was his character as a 'jealous God' " (19) but the phrase or title *'ēl qannô'* in Nahum is the only occurrence of it in the prophetical books, and then in an old psalm which has been adapted and used as an introduction to the prophecy. *qn'* can have both the notion of " jealousy " and the notion of " zeal " (cf. LXX *zēlōtēs*). Dahood compares Ps. 69 : 10, *qin'at bêt^ekā* " zeal for your house ", and *UT*, 52 : 21-22, *iqnu šmt [b]n šrm*, " I am zealous for the names of the Princes ". (20) In the title *'ēl qannô'*, *qannô'*, " jealous " seems to include a shade of meaning close to " furious, angry ". A number of Biblical texts are worth listing for they contain the same vocabulary of " wrath " as vv. 2-3 of Nahum 1. Cf. Num. 25 : 11 ; Deut. 6 : 15 ; 29 : 19 ; Is. 59 : 17 ; Ezek. 5 : 13 ; 8 : 3,5 ; 16 : 38,42 ; 23 : 25 ; 24 : 8 ; 36 : 6 ; 38 : 18-19. Note Zech. 8 : 2, *qinnē'tî l^eṣiyyôn qin'āh g^edôlāh w^eḥēmāh g^edôlāh qinnē'tî lāh*, " I am jealous for Zion with great jealousy and I am jealous for her with great wrath ", where the pair *qin'āh/ḥēmāh* matches the pair *qannô'/ḥēmāh* in Nahum. Recently, D. N. Freedman has rendered *qin'āh* by " fury " in Is. 42 : 13. (21)

nōqēm yahweh : " avenging is Yahweh ". The second *nōqēm yahweh* has frequently been expelled from the text by critics, following important MSS of the LXX. (22) But to do this is to ruin a finely structured bicolon, in which each colon has four stresses and where the syllable count is 8/9. It would also destroy a beautiful example of *chiasmus*.

(16) *UT*, Glossary No. 2246.

(17) Cf. *UT*, § 5.17. Note also R. Meyer, *Hebräische Grammatik* I, pp. 102 f.

(18) *UHP* 8. Cf. also M. Pope, *JBL* 85 (1966) 456.

(19) *From the Stone Age*, p. 309.

(20) *Psalms II*, p. 158.

(21) *CBQ* 30 (1968) 225-226.

(22) For the LXX evidence, see J. Ziegler, (ed.) *Septuaginta, Duodecim prophetae*, p. 253.

'l qnw' wnqm yhwh
nqm yhwh wbʿl ḥmh

Compare *UT*, 1 Aqht : 148-150,

knp nšrm bʿl yṯbr
bʿl yṯbr diy hmt

The wings of the eagles may Baʿal break
May Baʿal break the pinions of them.

ûbaʿal ḥēmāh : " and a Lord of wrath ". *baʿal ḥēmāh* is usually rendered " wrathful " or its equivalent. In Prov. 29 : 22 it balances *'îš 'ap*, " an angry man ", and in Prov. 22 : 24 and Sir. 8 : 16, *baʿal 'āp* is balanced by *'îš ḥēmôt. baʿal* is often found as a *Formwort.* For example : Prov. 23 : 2, *baʿal nepeš,* " man of big appetite " ; Prov. 24 : 8, *baʿal mᵉzimmôt,* " mischiefmaker " ; Eccles. 10 : 11, *baʿal hallāšôn,* " charmer ". For further examples consult Gen. 37 : 19 ; Exod. 24 : 14 ; Is. 41 : 15 ; 50 : 8 ; Prov 1 : 17 ; 18 : 9 ; Eccles. 10 : 20 ; Dan. 8 : 6,20 ; Sir. 6 : 6 ; 9 : 16.

W. R. Arnold believes that one should compare *baʿal ḥēmāh* with Ar. *ḏû*, " possessor of ". (23) However it seems to the present writer that *baʿal* should preferably be translated " Lord of..." in this verse of Nahum. The poet has deliberately balanced *'ēl qannô'* by *baʿal ḥēmāh.* Most informative for an understanding of these verses of Nahum is the Akkadian *ludlul bēl nēmeqi.* (24) In the latter poem one finds in line 1 of Table I :

[lud-lul] be-lu₄ né-me-qí *ilu [muštālum?]*

I will praise the lord of wisdom, the [deliberative?] god,
and in line 3 :

[ᵈ]marduk bēl né-me-qí *[ilu mu]š?-t[a?-lum?]*
Marduk, the lord of wisdom, the [deliberative?] god

Thus *bēl/ilu* might be profitably compared to *baʿal/'ēl,* and *bēl nēmeqi* to *baʿal ḥēmāh.* We shall return to this Babylonian text in the discussion of v. 3.

R. Tournay has also noticed " la mention parallèle de El et de Baal au v. 2 ", (25) and commenting generally on the hymn in Nah. 1,

(23) *ZAW* 21 (1901) 245.

(24) The lines we shall refer to specifically are found in the " Addenda " of W. G. Lambert, *Babylonian Wisdom Literature*, pp. 343-344.

(25) *RB* 65 (1958) 330.

asserts that the tradition about the flood and the Sinai events and the oracles of earlier prophets are as much the sources for this picture of Yahweh in the psalm. Tournay is clearly anxious that one should not draw any firm conclusions from the names " El " and " Baal ". To be sure, *'ēl* and *ba'al* are probably appellatives here in the Book of Nahum. On the other hand, the picture of Yahweh in these verses of Nah. 1 is very close to that of the Canaanite storm-god Ba'al, and in fact T. H. Gaster (26) and J. Gray (27) regard the hymn in Nah. 1 as basically a Canaanite poem of Ba'al. Albright has pointed out that since Gideon's father was called Joash, a Yahwist name, but Gideon himself bore the name Jerubbaal, there existed uncertainty as to whether Yahweh could be called Ba'al in that early period. (28) P. Miller, (29) discussing the relationship of Yahweh to Baal and El, believes that Baal and El shared certain characteristics. M. Pope (30) on the other hand, having noted that in Ugaritic literature El is described as a kindly one (cf. his title *ltpn il dpid*, " Lṭpn, god of kindness "), points out that Ba'al finally superseded El in the Canaanite pantheon. Yet the two names do occur in parallelism and one often wonders if the Canaanites themselves always made definitive distinctions. The two gods seem to be distinguished in texts like *UT*, 1 : 7, *dr il wp*[*ḫ*]*r b'l*, " The assemblage of El and congregation of Ba'al " ; 2 Aqht : I : 32-33, *bt b'l/bt il.* Cf. also, 2 Aqht : II : 21-22. Not so clear however is the problem of *ba'al b^erît* in Judg. 8 : 33 and 9 : 4, but *'ēl b^erît* in Judg. 9 : 46. R. E. Clements (31) in a recent discussion takes *'ēl b^erît* as simply an alternative for *ba'al b^erît*, with *'ēl* used in a purely appellative sense. Alternatively he thinks an earlier widespread *'ēl* religion gave place to a more active Baal religion in N. Palestine. H. Ringgren (32) is probably right in making *ba'al b^erît* identical with *'ēl b^erît.*

Perhaps no less interesting are the following Northwest Semitic names :

(26) *Thespis*, p. 143 ; *idem*, *Myth, Legend, and Custom in the Old Testament*, pp. 662-663.

(27) *VT* 6 (1956) 280 ; *idem*, *VT* 11 (1961) 16-17.

(28) *Yahweh*, pp. 199-200. Cf. his earlier discussion in *Archaeology and the Religion of Israel*, p. 113.

(29) *HTR* 60 (1967) 428-431.

(30) *El in the Ugaritic Texts*, p. 44.

(31) *JSS* 13 (1968) 21-32.

(32) *Israelite Religion*, p. 42, note 6.

Ugaritic Personal names : (33)

amril (34)		*amrbʿl*
ʿbdil		*ʿbdbʿl*

Divine Names :

ydbil	*ydbhd*	*ydbbʿl*
yrǵmil		*yrǵmbʿl*

Hebrew Personal Names : (35)

'elḥānān (2 Sam. 21 : 19)	*baʿal ḥānān* (36) (Gen. 36 : 38 f.)
'elyādāʿ (2 Sam. 5 : 16)	*beʿelyādāʿ* (1 Chron. 14 : 7)
'ēliyyāhû (1 Kings 17 : 1 f.)	*beʿalyāh* (1 Chron. 12 : 6)

beʿalyāh = " Yahweh is Baal (Lord) ! "

Phoenician : Compare *'lbʿl*, name of a king of Byblos (cf. *KAI*, 6 and 7) and the Ugar. personal name *ilbʿl* (*UT*, Glossary No. 163).

wenôṭēr hû' : " and he rages ". Not a few scholars have related Heb. *nāṭar* to Akk. *nadāru*, " to be angry, furious ; to rage ". At first, Köhler–Baumgartner (37) in the *Lexicon* posited a *nṭr* II and followed Driver (38) in making it cognate with Akk. *nadāru*. However, in the *Supplementum* to the *Lexicon*, that decision is reversed *sic* : " *nṭr* II potius = I, omissio *'ap* ". (39) In Jer. 3 : 5 and Amos 1 : 11, *nṭr* is paralleled by *šmr*, and Driver would relate the latter verb in Jer. 3 : 5 to Akk. *šamāru*, " to rage ". (40) Hence he equates *nṭr* – *šmr* in Jer. 3 : 5 with Akk. *nadāru* – *šamāru*. His proposal has been accepted

(33) Cf. the List of names in *UT*, pp. 508-522 ; also *Supplement to the Ugaritic Textbook* No. 1073a ; F. Gröndahl, *Die Personennamen der Texte aus Ugarit* pp. 104-105.

(34) The Heb. name *'mryhw* occurs on a seal found at the site of ancient Kiryat Yeʿarim near Jerusalem. Cf. N. Avigad, *IEJ* 13 (1963) 324. Avigad also refers to a seal from Megiddo with the name *'l'mr*. More recently, the same scholar has published a seal reading : *l'mr'l bn ynḥm*. See his article, " Ammonite and Moabite Seals ", in *Near Eastern Archaeology in the Twentieth Century : Essays in Honor of Nelson Glueck*, edited by J. A. Sanders, p. 286.

(35) Cf. M. Noth, *Personennamen*, for all these names.

(36) *bʿl ḥn* appears on a 7th century B. C. Hebrew seal. Cf. R. Giveon, *PEQ* 93 (1961) 42.

(37) KB 613.

(38) *JTS* 32 (1931) 361-363.

(39) *Supplementum ad Lexicon in Veteris Testamenti Libros* p. 172.,

(40) *JTS* 32 (1931) 362.

also by D. Winton Thomas (41) and most recently upheld by M. Held, (42) who goes a step further than Driver and sees the same pair of verbs in Amos 1 : 11, which he reads (on the basis of the Syr.) *wyṭr lʿd ʾpw wʿbrth šmrh nṣḥ* and renders : " And his anger seethed forever, his wrath raged for eternity ". Recently, Held has made a detailed presentation of the case for Heb. *nṭr* II = Akk. **ndr* and it is certainly impressive. (43) It is not necessary to repeat the details here, but Held makes the following important points. One must distinguish *šmr/nṣr*, " to guard, watch " from *šmr* II / *nṭr* II, " to rage, to be in a fury ". The latter pair of verbs " are statives and are generally employed without an object ". (44) *šmr/nṣr* however are transitive and take an object. Held also gives a plausible explanation for the shift *d* > *ṭ* in *ndr* – *nṭr*. He suggests that there has been an internal Akk. development and points to Akk. *durru/ṭurru*, " rope ", and *derû/ṭerû*, " to cane, thrash ", as examples. (45) He does not rule out the possibility that the shift may have taken place in Hebrew under the influence of Aram. *nṭr*, " to guard ". (46)

The pair *nṭr/nqm* is found in Lev. 19 : 18, *lōʾ tiqqōm wᵉlōʾ tiṭṭōr ʾet bᵉnê ʿammekā*, " You shall not take vengeance or rage against the sons of your people ". In Is. 1 : 24, *hôy ʾennāḥēm miṣṣāray wᵉʾinnāqᵉmāh mēʾôyᵉbāy*, " Ah ! I will vent my wrath on my enemies, and avenge myself on my foes ", the parallelism of *mēʾôyᵉbāy//miṣṣāray*

(41) In *Record and Revelation*, p. 394.

(42) *Eretz Israel* 9 (1969) 73 n. 19.

(43) *ANES* 3 (1971) 46-55.

(44) *Ibid.* 48.

(45) *Ibid.* 54-55.

(46) This Aram. *nṭr* " to guard " is of course a cognate of Heb. *nṭr* I " to guard ". Heb. *nṭr* I occurs four times in the Canticle of Canticles (Cant. 1 : 6 [twice] ; 8 : 11,12). Though frequently labelled an Aramaism, Heb. *nṭr* I may in fact be a dialectical form of *nṣr*. All the more so, because in Ugar. one finds both *ḥẓr* and *ḥṭr* (Aram. *ḥwṭrʾ*) with which Heb. *ḥṣr*, " court ", is cognate. Virolleaud (*Ugaritica V*, p. 550) takes Ugar. *ḥṭr* as dialectical for *ḥdr*, " room ", but the parallelism with *bt*, " house " makes the meaning of *ḥṭr* clear as has been pointed out by Gordon in the *Supplement* to *UT*, § 19. 852a ; Dahood, *Psalms III*, p. 259 ; J. Blau and J. C. Greenfield, *BASOR* 200 (1970) 11. The Heb.-Phoen. pair *bt/ḥṣr* and Ugar. *bt/ḥẓr* have been dealt with elsewhere by the present writer ; cf. *Biblica* 49 (1968) 513 n. 2, and Dahood, *Psalms II*, p. 282.

Regarding Aram. *nṭr* " to guard ", the Aramaic specialist Fitzmyer mentions that it begins to appear at Elephantine. Cf. his articles, in *JAOS* 81 (1961) 202 ; and *Biblica* 46 (1965) 54. For further discussion of Aram. *nṭr*, consult O. Rössler, *ZAW* 74 (1962) 26 ; M. Wagner, *Aramaismen*, pp. 83-84 ; J. Blau, in *In Memoriam Paul Kahle*, pp. 41-42.

matches that of *l*^{e}*ōy*^{e}*bāyw*/*l*^{e}*ṣārāyw* in Nahum. For further comment, see the remarks on v. 9 below, where the Ugar. pair *ib*//*ṣrt* is discussed.

M. Held compares the *nṭr l* in Nahum with Akk. *nadāru ana.* (47)

1:3

'erek 'appayim ûg^{e}*dol kōaḥ :* " slow to anger but great in power ". This should be compared with Ps. 145 : 8, *'erek 'appayim ûg*^{e}*dol ḥāsed,* " slow to anger and great in kindness ". *'erek 'appayim* (48) pairs off with *rab ḥesed* in Exod. 34 : 6 ; Num. 14 : 18 ; Joel 2 : 13 ; Ps. 86 : 15 ; 103 : 8 ; Neh. 9 : 17. In Ps. 147 : 5, *rab kōaḥ* is found. With this kind of phrase, A. Haldar (49) compares *UT*, 127 : 34,47, *qṣr npš*, " wretched " (Haldar's version). M. Held (50) however, commenting on Heb. *qṣr*(*h*) *rwḥ* and *qṣr*(*h*) *npš* (cf. Num. 21 : 4 and Zech. 11 : 8), compares the latter phrase with Ugar. *qṣr npš* and Akk. *karû ša ikki* (*napišti*), " impatience, irritability ", the opposite of Akk. *arāku ša ikki* (= Heb. *'erek rûaḥ*). (51)

Compare the following :

'erek 'appayim	*q*^{e}*ṣar 'appayim* (Prov. 14 : 17)
'erek rûaḥ (Eccles. 7 : 8) (52)	*q*^{e}*ṣar rûaḥ* (Prov. 14 : 29)
'ōrek rûaḥ (Sir. 5 : 11)	*qōṣer rûaḥ* (Exod. 6 : 9)
Phoen. *'rkrḥ* (CIS, I: 97)	*qṣr rḥ* (CIS, I: 100)
'ōrek yāmîm (e.g. Ps. 21 : 5)	*q*^{e}*ṣar yāmîm* (Job 14 : 1)
Ugar. *urk ym* (*UT*, 1018 : 20)	
Phoen. *'rk ymm* (*KAI*, 26 : AIII : 5)	

(47) *ANES* 3 (1971) 48. It should be mentioned that some South Semitic words have been associated with Akk. *nadāru.* Cf. W. Leslau, *JAOS* 89 (1969) 21.

(48) On this phrase, cf. GK § 128x.

(49) *Studies*, p. 17.

(50) *Eretz-Israel* 9 (1969) 78-79 n. 69.

(51) On both the Akk. and Hebrew, cf. *CAD* [I/J] 59-60. Note for example *ikki ša bēlīja līrikši*, " may my lord have patience ".

(52) Dahood notes that *'erek rûaḥ* is used by Eccles. in place of normal *'erek 'appayim* and attributes this to Phoenician influence. Cf. *Biblica* 33 (1952) 208-209.

'erek hā'ēber (Ezek. 17 : 3)
g^e^dôl hakk^e^nāpîm (Ezek. 17 : 3)
Ugar. *rḥb mknpt* (*UT* 125 : 9,109) ([53])

w^e^naqqēh lō' y^e^naqqeh yahweh : " and Yahweh will certainly not acquit (the guilty) ". A. Haldar ([54]) takes MT *lō'* as a misunderstood emphatic lamed and finds support in Jer. 4 : 27, *š^e^māmāh tiyheh kol hā'āreṣ w^e^kālāh lō' 'e'^e^śeh*, a text where J. A. Soggin ([55]) also reads *lō'* as an emphatic lamed. Soggin translates it : " Tutta la regione diverrà deserta ; certo ne farò uno scempio totale ". ([56]) Yet even if this reading of the Jeremiah text is correct, a negative meaning of *lō'* makes the only good sense in Nahum, especially in view of Exod. 34 : 7 and Num. 14 : 18, where we find the same phrase — *w^e^naqqēh lō' y^e^naqqeh.* Note also Jer. 30 : 11 ; 46 : 28, *w^e^naqqēh lō' 'ᵃnaqq^e^kā*, " And I will certainly not let you go unpunished ". In the Niphal form, *nqh* means " to be innocent, free ", and in the Piel, " to acquit, let free ; spare from punishment ". A 7th cent. B.C. extra-biblical Hebrew attestation of the root is found in the Yavneh-Yam inscription, *KAI*, 200 : 11. Much more interesting however is Inscription B of the Cave inscriptions from Khirbet Beit Lei, as read by F. M. Cross : ([57])

nqh yh 'l ḥnn. nqh yh yhwh
Absolve (us) O Merciful God!
Absolve (us) O Yahweh!

Compare Exod. 34 : 6, *yhwh 'l rḥwm wḥnwn 'rk 'pym wrb ḥsd w'mt ... wnqh l' ynqh.* A similar list of attributes is found in Num. 14 : 18 ; Ps. 86 : 15 ; 103 : 8 ; 145 : 8 ; Joel 2 : 13. In Exod. 34 : 14, the sequence to Exod. 34 : 6 f., the titles *yahweh qannā'* and *'ēl qannā'* are found. W. Beyerlin sees the sequence as " a well-established liturgical sequence ". ([58]) However, despite the title *'ēl qannô'* in Nah. 1 : 2,

([53]) Cf. Dahood, *Psalms III*, pp. 44-45, where he compares Ps. 104 : 25, *r^e^ḥab yādāyim*, " broad of reach ", with *UT*, 125 : 9, *rḥb mknpt*, " broad of wingspan " describing Ba'al. He also notes *UT*, 2 Aqht : V : 24-25, *dḥrš ydm*, " the one skillful of hands ".

([54]) *Studies*, p. 18.

([55]) *Biblica* 46 (1965) 56-59. Soggin suggests however (p. 59) that an ' could be suppressed (dittography) in *l' "śh.*

For an interpretation of *lō'* as a negative in Jer. 4 : 27, cf. Bright, *Jeremiah*, p. 33.

([56]) *Biblica* 46 (1965) 59.

([57]) In *Near Eastern Archaeology in the Twentieth Century : Essays in Honor of Nelson Glueck*, pp. 299-306.

([58]) *Origins and History of the Oldest Sinaitic Traditions* (Oxford 1965) p. 138.

he regards *yahweh 'erek 'appayim ûgᵉdol kōaḥ wᵉnaqqēh lō' yᵉnaqqeh yahweh*, as a gloss. Is it really surprising however to find words which sum up the Covenant theology of southern Israel in Nahum? After all, Nahum was probably in Judah!

The *NEB* also regards Nah. 1 : 3a as a gloss (?) or insertion. Because it rendered *baʿal ḥēmāh* in 1 : 2, by "quick to anger", it would obviously have to regard *'erek 'appayim*, "slow to anger", as a contradiction, and therefore take that part of the verse as an insertion, just as many critics had believed it was anyway.

We have already insisted above that *baʿal ḥēmāh* is better rendered by "Lord of wrath". Furthermore, *'erek 'appayim*, "slow to anger" is not inconsistency in the description of the "Lord of wrath". Compare the following lines from the Babylonian *ludlul bēl nēmeqi*, already referred to above:

3	[^{d}]*marduk bēl né-me-qí*	[*ilu mu*]*š?-t*[*a?-lum?*]
4	[*mu?-ṣ*]*a?-bít mu-ši*	*mu-pa-áš-šir ur-r*[*u*]
5	[*š*]*á ki-ma* u_4*-mi me-ḫe-e*	*la-mu-u ug-gat-su*
6	*ù ki-i ma-ni-ti še-ri*	*za-aq-šú ṭābu* (dùg.ga)
7	*uz-zu-uš-šú la ma-ḫar*	*a-bu-bu ru-ub-šú*
8	*mu-us-saḫ-ḫir ka-ras-su*	*ka-bat-ta-šú ta-a-a-rat*
9	*šá naq-bi qātē-šú*	*la i-na-áš-š*[*u*]*-u šá-ma-'u*
10	*rit-tuš rab-bat*	*ú-k*[*aš*]*-šú mi-tu*!

3 Marduk, the Lord of wisdom, the [deliberative god,]
4 Who lays hold on the night, but lets free the day,
5 Whose fury surrounds him like the blast of a tornado,
6 Yet whose breeze is as pleasant as a morning zephyr,
7 His anger is irresistible, his rage is a hurricane,
8 But his heart is merciful, his mind forgiving,
9 The ... of whose hands the heavens cannot hold back,
10 But whose gentle hand sustains the moribund, (59)

Commenting on *ú-k*[*aš*]*-šú* in line 10, W. G. Lambert notes that *kâšu* has two related meanings, probably from same root: (i) tarry, be late; (ii) be kind — the latter perhaps having the implication of "slow to anger". (60)

The series of cola in verses in Nah. 1 : 2-3a features the juxtaposition of the consonants *n* and *q* no fewer than six times: *qnw' wnqm*/*nqm* (twice)/*wnqh* – *ynqh*. In *qannô'* there is duplication of *n*;

(59) Text and translation from W. G. Lambert, *Babylonian Wisdom Literature*, pp. 343-344.
(60) *Ibid.*, p. 344.

in *wᵉnaqqēh lōʾ yᵉnaqqeh*, duplication of *q*. Anyone who might be concerned about the repetition of the phrase *nōqēm yahweh* should consider the pertinent remarks of J. Muilenburg : " Repetition serves to center the thought, to rescue it from disparateness and diffuseness, to focus the richness of varied prediction upon the poet's controlling concern .... Repetition serves too to give continuity to the writer's thought ; the repeated word or phrase is often strategically located, thus providing a clue to the movement and stress of the poem ". ([61])

bᵉsûpāh ûbiśᵉʿārāh darkô : " In the whirlwind and in the storm is his way ". The pair *sûpāh/sᵉʿārāh* is found in Is. 29 : 6 ; and Ps. 83 : 16 has *sûpāh/saʿar*. The spelling *śᵉʿārāh* (with *ś* instead of *s*) is found in Job 4 : 15 ([62]) and 9 : 17. Note also in Is. 28 : 2, *śaʿar* for the more usual *saʿar*. The verb from the root occurs frequently with both spellings. *śᵉʿārāh* is related to Akk. *šāru*, " wind ".

The LXX went astray in rendering *bᵉsûpāh* by *en sunteleía*, presumably connecting *sûpāh* with *sôp*, " end ". Cf. also Amos 1 : 14, *bᵉyôm sûpāh*, LXX, *en hēméra sunteleías autēs.*

As M. Pope points out, the ancient cult of the weather god explains the common connection of a theophany with storms and other " metereological phenomena " ([63]). Compare the following theophanies : Is. 29 : 6, *mēʿim yahweh ṣᵉbāʾôt tippāqēd bᵉraʿam ûbᵉraʿaš wᵉqôl gādôl sûpāh ûsᵉʿārāh wᵉlahab ʾēš ʾôkēlāh*, " You will be visited by Yahweh Sabaot with thunder and earthquake and great noise, with whirl wind and storm and a flame of devouring fire " ; Is. 66 : 15, *kî hinnēh yahweh bāʾēš yābôʾ wᵉkassûpāh markᵉbōtāyw lᵉhāšîb bᵉḥēmāh ʾappô wᵉgaʿᵃrātô bᵉlahᵃbê ʾēš*, " For Yahweh will come in fire and his chariots like the whirlwind, to return his anger in fury and his rebuke with flames of fire ". Yahweh is described as walking in the tempests in Zech. 9 : 14, *wᵉyahweh baššôpār yitqāʿ wᵉhālak bᵉsaʿᵃrôt têmān*, " And Yahweh will blow the trumpet and march forth in the tempests of the south ". With the tempest, Yahweh " blows " (Is. 40 : 24) ; " scatters " (Zech. 7 : 14). Jer. 23 : 19 (= 30 : 23) mentions the " storm of Yahweh " (*saʿᵃrat yahweh*).

wᵉʿānān ʾᵃbaq raglāyw : " and the clouds are the dust of his feet ". This should be compared with Ps. 18 : 10, *waʿᵃrāpel taḥat raglāyw*, " a storm-cloud under his feet ". The mention of clouds and

([61]) *Congress Volume* (VTS 1 ; Leiden 1953), p. 99.

([62]) Cf. Dahood, *Biblica* 48 (1967) 544-545. Dahood repoints MT *śaʿᵃrat* to *śᵉʿārāt* and explains *śᵉʿārāt* as a fem. absolute singular with the ending *-t*, as in Ugar. and Phoen.

([63]) Pope, *Job*, pp. 249 f. (note on " storm ").

the allusion to Yahweh's chariots in Is. 66 : 15 (quoted above), recall the divine title, *rōkēb ba'ᵃrābôt* (Ps. 68 : 5), Ugar. *rkb 'rpt*, " Rider of the Clouds ". (64) See also Is. 14 : 14, *'e'ᵉleh 'al bomᵒtê 'āb 'eddammeh lᵉ'elyôn*, " I will go upon the backs of the clouds, I will make myself like the Most High ". J. Gray (65) pertinently refers to the words addressed to Ba'al in *UT*, 67 : V : 6-7, *wat qḥ 'rptk rḥk mdlk mṭrtk*, " Thou, take thy clouds, thy wind, thy rain-cloud, thy rain " (Gray's translation). (66) In the Assyrian recension of Atraḫasis, the Babylonian story of the flood, Adad is described as riding on the winds !

ᵈAdad ina šār erbetti irtakab parē[*šu*]

Adad rode on the four winds, [his] asses. (67)

1 : 4

gô'ēr bayyām : " He rebukes ". The construction *g'r b* occurs in *UT*, 137 : 24, *bhm yg'r b'l*, " Baal rebukes them ". In *UT*, 56 : 23, *k yg'r* [*ssw*], " If the horse roars ", one has more evidence to support the alternative renderings of Heb. *g'r*, suggested by H. G. May. (68) The translation " roars " is suggested for this Nahum verse by an examination of texts like Ps. 18 : 16, *wayyērā'û 'ᵃpîqê mayim wayyiggālû môsᵉdôt tēbēl migga'ᵃrātᵉkā yahweh minnišmat rûaḥ 'appekā*, " the fountains of the sea were exposed, and the world's foundations were laid bare, At your roar, O Yahweh, at the blast from your nostrils"(69)

(64) Opposition to the interpretation of *rkb 'rpt* as " cloud-gatherer " has been expressed elsewhere. Cf. my article " *Trkb qmḥ* in the Arad Ostracon and Biblical Hebrew *rekeb*, ' upper millstone ' ", *VT* 19 (1969) 121-122. Cf. also W. L. Moran, *Biblica* 43 (1962) 323 ff.

(65) *VT* 11 (1961) 16.

(66) The precise meaning of Ugar. *mdl* is not clear. Dahood has recently suggested that on the basis of Ps. 135 : 7, *mdl* may mean " lightning ". Ps. 135 : 7 contains *nᵉśī'îm*, " clouds ", *bᵉrāqîm*, " lightning ", *lammāṭār*, " rain ", and *rûaḥ*, " wind ", to which would answer in *UT*, 67 : V : 6-7, *'rptk*, " your clouds " ; *mdlk* " your lightning ", *mṭrk*, your rain ", and *rḥk*, " your wind ". Cf. his article in *Ugarit-Forschungen* 1 (1969) 35, *Psalms III*, p. 261.

Dahood had previously taken *mdl* to mean " rain-cloud ". Cf. " Ugaritic Lexicography ", in *Mélanges Eugene Tisserant I*, p. 87, where he points to *mdl* parallel to *šḥq* in Is. 40 : 15. Amongst other discussions note J. C. de Moor, *ZAW* 78 (1966) 69-71, who relates Ugar. *mdl* to Sum. *mudul*, Akk. *mudulu*, " bar, rod " ; and A. A. Wieder, *JBL* 84 (1965) 164.

(67) Text and translation from W. G. Lambert and A. R. Millard, *Atra-Ḫasīs : The Babylonian Story of the Flood*, p. 123.

(68) *JBL* 74 (1955) 17 n. 32.

(69) Dahood, *Psalms I*, p. 102 and notes on p. 110.

Ps. 104 : 7, *min gaʿarātekā yenûsûn min qôl raʿamekā yeḥāpēzûn*, " At your roar they fled, at your thunderous voice they took to flight ".([70]) But the present writer prefers the more traditional " rebuke " in Is. 50 : 2, *hēn begaʿarātî ʾaḥarîb yām ʾāśîm nehārôt midbār*, " Behold by my rebuke I made the sea parched, I made the rivers a desert " ; and therefore " rebukes the sea " in Nahum. Cf. the *NEB*.

Notice the vocabulary of Is. 50 : 2 above (*gʿr/ḥrb/ym/nhr*) and in Ps. 106 : 9, *wayyigʿar beyam sûp wayyeḥerāb*, " He rebuked the Sea of Reeds, and dried it up ". In Nahum too we have *gʿr/ym/nhr/ḥrb*

bayyām ... hannehārôt : " the sea ... the rivers ". The pairs *yām, yammîm/nāhār, nehārôt* are frequent in biblical poetry ; cf. Is. 48 : 18 ; 50 : 2 ; Ps. 24 : 2 ; 66 : 6 ; 72 : 8 ; 80 : 12 ; 89 : 26 ; 98 : 7-8 ; Hab. 3 : 8. The parallelism between *ym* and *nhr* is found in Ugaritic poetry also. Thus *UT*, 68 : 16-17, *ylm ktp zbl ym bn ydm ṯpṭ nhr*, " It strikes the back (shoulders) of Prince Sea, Between the arms of Judge River " ; *UT*, 68 : 19-20, *mr ym lksih nhr lkḥṯ drkth*, " Drive Sea from his throne, River from his seat of dominion ". Further examples are *UT*, 51 : II : 6-7 ; 68 : 12-13,14-15,21-22,24-25,27,29-30 ; 129 : 7,9,21,23 ; 137 22,26,28,30,33-34,41,44 ; ʿnt : III : 36.

nehārôt might possibly be rendered " ocean-currents ", a meaning fairly established in Ps. 24 : 2, *kî hûʾ ʿal yammîm yesādāh weʿal nehārôt yekônenehā*, " For he based it upon the seas, established it upon the ocean-currents " ; ([71]) Jon. 2 : 4, *wenāhār yesōbebēnî*, " and the ocean-currents surround me " ; Is. 44 : 27, *hāʾōmēr laṣṣûlāh ḥorābî wenaharōtayik ʾôbîš*, " who says to the deep ' Be parched, I will make your currents dry ' ".

wayyabbešēhû ... heḥerîb : " and dries it up ... he parches ". Gaster ([72]) regards *wayyabbešēhû* and the succeeding verbs as being all in the past tense and referring therefore to mythical events of the past. It is true that in Ps. 74 : 13 f., for example, there is a description of an event from the past, viz. Yahweh's victory over the forces of Chaos. In Nahum however the introductory psalm is descriptive and the verbs are better rendered as presents.

The parallelism of *ybš* and *ḥrb* is found in chiastic Is. 42 : 15, *ʾaḥarîb hārîm ûgebāʿôt wekol ʿeśbām ʾôbîš*, " I will lay waste mountains

([70]) *Ibid.*

([71]) Translation of Dahood, *Psalms I*, p. 150. Cf. his notes on p. 151, where he refers to the works of A. R. Johnson, *Sacral Kingship in Ancient Israel* (Cardiff 1955) and W. H. Schmidt, *Königtum Gottes in Ugarit und Israel* (Berlin 1961).

([72]) *Myth, Legend, and Custom in the Old Testament*, p. 663.

and hills, and all their vegetation I will dry up ", and in Jer. 51 : 36, *w^{e}hah^{a}rabtî 'et yammāh w^{e}hōbaštî 'et m^{e}qôrāh,* " And I will parch her sea and I will dry up her fountain ". Cf. also Is. 44 : 27.

Notice the play on the consonants *b* and *y* in *bayyām wayyabb^{e}šēhû.* No less noteworthy is the repetition of the consonants in *UT*, 68 : 17, *ym lymk,* " Sea does not collapse ".

bāšān w^{e}karmel ... l^{e}bānôn : " Bashan and Carmel ... Lebanon ". Bashan of course is the fertile land east of Jordan, south of Mt. Hermon and east of the Sea of Galilee. Carmel is a promontory terminating the central range of Palestine. Lebanon is a chain of mountains extending N-S along the coast of Syria. It was famous for its cedars. Compare Ps. 29 : 5-6, which mentions *'arzê hall^{e}bānôn,* " the cedars of Lebanon ", and *UT*, 51 : VI : 20-21, *llbnn w'ṣh lšryn mḥmd arzh,* " to Lebanon and its trees, to Shirion and its choicest cedars ". Cf. also Is. 2 : 13, where the " cedars of Lebanon " are balanced by the "strong oaks of Bashan ", and Ez. 27 : 6, which informs us that Tyre made oars for its ships from Bashan oak timber. All three places are mentioned in a context similar to that in Nahum in Is. 33 : 9, *'ābal 'uml^{e}lāh 'āreṣ heḥpîr l^{e}bānôn qāmal hāyāh haššārôn kā'^{a}rābāh w^{e}nō'ēr bāšān w^{e}karmel,* " The land mourns and languishes ; Lebanon is confounded and withers away ; Sharon is like a desert ; and Bashan and Carmel shake off their leaves ". In Jer. 22 : 20, Bashan balances Lebanon, and they are a pair in Jer. 50 : 19. According to W. F. Albright, the place name Bashan may originally have had something to do with " vipers " in view of Ugar. *bṯn*, Akk. *bašmu*, Heb. *peten.* ([73])

'umlal ... 'umlāl : " wither ... withers ". The first *'umlal* is frequently altered by critics to a verb of which the initial letter is *d*, in order to restore an acrostic. ([74]) The apparatus of *BH*[3] illustrates the diversity of opinions as to what verb is supposed to be in the text in place of *'umlal.* The LXX *ōligōthē* (the second *'mll* is rendered *exélipe*) is not conclusive evidence for a different reading. Even if one were to argue for a confusion in the Old Hebrew–Phoenician script between 𐤀 (') and Δ (*d*), there is still a *m* to be accounted for. 4QpNah has *'mll* twice also. It is quite possible that the desire for repetition in the chiasm overcame the needs of the acrostic. The

([73]) W. F. Albright, *HUCA* 23 (1950-51) 27. Note also, J. A. Fitzmyer, *JAOS* 81 (1961) 198, for Sefîre Aram. *btn*, but later Aram. *pitnā'*, Syr. *patnā'*. Cf. also Dahood, *Psalms II*, p. 145.

([74]) Recently, for example, R. Tournay, *RB* 65 (1958) 330 ; Gaster, *Myth, Legend, and Custom*, p. 727 n. 16. Where does Gaster obtain *'umlallū* (*sic* !) ?

repetition of the verb *'umlal* is not contrary to Hebrew style. M. Dahood, commenting on the repetition of *yᵉdabbᵉrû* in Ps. 73 : 8, points to a parallel in *UT*, 2 Aqht : V : 31-33, *tbʿ kṯr lahlh hyn tbʿ lmšknth*, " Kothar departs for his tent, Hayyin departs for his habitation ".(75)

1:5

hārîm ... wᵉhaggᵉbāʿôt : " The mountains ... and the hills ". The parallelism and the collocation of *har* and *gibʿāh* are very frequent in the Old Testament and especially in Isaiah. (76) In Ugar., *gbʿ* (= Heb. *gebaʿ*), " hill ", is often parallel with *ǧr* (Heb. *ṣûr*), " mountain ". For example, *UT*, 51 : V : 77-78, *tblk ǧrm mid ksp gbʿm mḥmd ḫrṣ*, " The mountains shall bring you much silver, the hills choicest of gold " ; and *UT*, 67 : VI : 26-27, *kl ǧr lkbd arṣ kl gbʿ lkbd šdm*, " every mountain to the midst of the earth, every hill to the midst of the fields ". This Canaanite pairing of *ǧr* and *gbʿ* is found in Num. 23 : 9 (Blessing of Balaam), *kî mērōʾš ṣūrîm 'erʾennû ûmiggᵉbāʿôt 'ᵃšûrennû*, " For I see him from the top of the mountains, and I behold him from the hills ".

The question mark placed by *HALAT* 244a, before Ugar. *hr* can now be removed in view of *UT*, 608 : 7,9,19 *isp špš lhrm ǧrpl ʿl arṣ*, which is translated by C. H. Gordon thus : " The Sun's gathering from the mountains mist upon the earth ", (77) but is well rendered by Dahood : " The gathering of the sun upon the mountains, a dark cloud over the earth ". (78) EA 74 : 20 contains the Canaanite gloss *ḫarri*, " mountain region ". (79) Note the Heb. plural *gᵉbāʿôt*, but Ugar. *gbʿm*, and consult the comments below on Nah. 2 : 4, *pᵉlādôt*.

The Wadi Murabbaʿât scroll reads *hhrym* with the article, a reading long suggested by scholars on the basis of the LXX *tà orē*. The sense is not affected, though such a reading would give 9 syllables in each colon.

rāʿᵃšû ... hitmōgāgû : " shake ... melt away ". In v. 4 the effects of Yahweh's wrathful voice upon the sea, rivers and vegetation are set forth. In this verse and the following verse 6, the picture is that of the mountains and hills tottering and trembling. The roots *rʿš* and *mwg* frequently signify the shaking of the earth before Yahweh.

(75) *Psalms II*, p. 189 ; *idem*, *Ugarit-Forschungen* 1 (1969) 30-31.
(76) Cf. Deut. 12 : 2 ; 33 : 15 ; Is. 2 : 2,14 ; 10 : 32 ; 30 : 17, etc.
(77) *Supplement*, p. 551, § 19.790.
(78) *Biblica* 50 (1969) 356, *sub voce ʿᵃrāpel.*
(79) *CAD* [Ḫ] 115.

Thus Ps. 46 : 7, *nātan b^eqôlô tāmûg 'āreṣ*, " He gives forth his voice, the earth melts away " ; Joel 4 : 16, *w^eyahweh miṣṣiyyôn yiš'āg ûmîrûšālayim yittēn qôlô w^erā'^ašû šāmayim wā'āreṣ*, " And Yahweh roars from Zion, and gives forth his voice from Jerusalem, and the heavens and the earth shake ". Compare EA 147 : 14-15, *ša iddin rigmašu ina šamê kima addi ù ta[r]kub gabbi māti ištu rigmišu*, " who gives his voice from heaven like Haddu, and all the mountains quake at his voice ". Gaster (80) rightly compares also the badly damaged *UT*, 51 : VII : 31-35 which mentions Ba'al's voice shaking the earth accompanied by the quaking of the mountains and highlands. Dahood has compared the same Ugaritic text with Ps. 18 : 14, *wayyar'ēm baššāmayim yahweh w^e'elyôn yittēn qōlô*, " Yahweh thundered from the heavens, and the Most High gave forth his voice ". (81)

If there is little difficulty in defining *r'š*, the verb *mwg* is open to more discussion. Several translations (e.g. *RSV*) offer " melt " for *hitmōgāgû* and this seems to be right. One could choose the meaning " tremble " on the basis of Ar. *māğa*, " surge, be in tumult, totter "(82) a fitting parallel to " shake ". Cf. the *NEB*, " the hills heave and swell ". To support this interpretation, one could point to Jer. 4 : 24, *rā'îtî hehārîm w^ehinnēh rō'^ašîm w^ekol hagg^ebā'ôt hitqalqālû*, " I saw the mountains and lo they were quaking, And all the hills rocked to and fro ". (83) However, favouring the rendering " melt, melt away ", are such texts as Mic. 1 : 4, *w^enāmassû hehārîm taḥtāyw w^ehā'^amāqîm yitbaqqā'û kaddônag mipp^enê hā'ēš k^emayim muggārîm b^emôrād*, " And the mountains will melt under him and the valleys will be split, like wax before the fire, like waters poured down a steep place ", and Ps. 97 : 5, *hārîm kaddônag nāmassû*, " The mountains melt like wax ". The hithpolel of *mwg* only occurs in two other places, viz. Amos 9 : 13 and Ps. 107 : 26,. The combination of " quaking " and " melting " here in Nahum is somewhat like that of the concepts of " sweat " and " quaking " in *UT*, 'nt : III : 29-32. Cf. below, commentary on Nah. 2 : 11. Observe once again the repetition of a consonant (*g*) in *w^ehagg^ebā'ôt hitmōgāgû*. O. T. Allis (84) has rightly stressed the frequency of words in the Book of Nahum, which have a consonant repeated adjacently, and lists *hitmōgāgû* as an example.

(80) *Myth, Legend, and Custom*, p. 663.

(81) Dahood, *Psalms I*, p. 106, with reference also to *UT*, 51 : V : 70, *wtn qlh b'rpt*, " And he gave forth his voice from the clouds ".

(82) Cf. ZLH 416a.

(83) J. Bright, *Jeremiah*, p. 30.

(84) " Nahum, Nineveh, Elkosh ", *Evangelical Quarterly* 27 (1955) 73.

wattiššā' hā'āreṣ : " The earth is laid waste ". Reading *wattiššā'* from *šā'āh* (cf. *BH*^{3}). ZLH 534 retains MT *wattiśśā'*, and take it as eliptic for *nāśā' qôl.* In Ps. 89 : 10, *b*^{e}*śô' gallāyw* is rendered by Dahood : " when its waves surge " ; ([85]) MT *wattiśśā'* could therefore be kept and taken as intransitive. A. George unnecessarily alters the consonantal text and reads *wattāšaḥ* and renders it : " (la terre) s'effondre devant lui ". ([86]) The verb in question, *wattiššā'*, is *wayyiqtol*, and " is laid waste " fits the syntactic shape of a *wayyiqtol* after the " shake " and " melt away " in *qatal* in 5a, better than " surge ", or the other possible translations of the form without emendation of the *ś* in the root. ([87])

w^{e}*tēbēl w*^{e}*kol yōš*^{e}*bê bāh :* " the world and all who dwell in it ". W. F. Albright proposes a different version, and relates consonantal *wtbl w* to *'bl* ; hence he reads *wattêbal kol yôš*^{e}*bê bāh*, " and all its inhabitants drooped ". ([88]) He regards this reading and meaning as " proven " from parallels in Amos 8 : 8 and 9 : 15. W. L. Moran ([89]) points to Nah. 1 : 5 for an example of third plural masc. *taqtulû(na)* (hence *têbālû* for *tbl w*) which he believes probably occurs in Hebrew in the light of evidence from the El Amarna texts and from Ugaritic. This reading, he claims rightly, removes the necessity of rejecting the *w* (so Albright — *tbl* [*w*]*kl*) and of explaining the *t* preformative form as 3rd fem. sing. with plural subjects. Attractive as Moran's reading is, it seems better to retain the traditional rendering and interpretation of *tēbēl w*^{e}*yōš*^{e}*bê bāh.* This phrase and similar phrases parallel to *'ereṣ* are stock phrases in Hebrew poetry : cf. Is. 14 : 17 ; 18 : 3 ; 24 : 4 ; 26 : 9,18 ; 34 : 1 ; etc. L. I. J. Stadelmann ([90]), who has made a special study of the Hebrew " Parts of the world ", relates Heb. *tēbēl* to Akk. *tābalu* in the expression *eli tabali*, " by land ".

([85]) *Psalms II*, p. 314 with reference there to BDB 670-671.
([86]) *Michée, Sophonie, Nahum : La Sainte Bible.*
([87]) I am grateful to A. Cody for this observation regarding the syntax.
([88]) Albright, *CBQ* 7 (1945) 23.
Note also that K. Elliger, *Das Buch der zwölf kleinen Propheten II*, p. 4, reads *w*^{e}*'āb*^{e}*lû* (Horst) or *wayya'(a)b*^{e}*lû kol.*
([89]) In *BANE* pp. 62-63 and p. 71 n. 108. See also *JCS* 5 (1951) 33-35.
On the presence of *taqtulû(na)* in Hebrew, note the following : A. Alt, *ZAW* 60 (1944) 158-159 ; J. Friedrich, *Phönizisch–Punische Grammatik*, § 129 ; Driver, *CML* 130 ; Gordon, *UT*, § 9.14 ; Dahood, *PNWSP* 5 ; *idem*, *UHP* 38 ; T. F. McDaniel, *Biblica* 49 (1968) 213-215.
([90]) *The Hebrew Conception of the World*, pp. 129-130.

1 : 6

lipnê zaʿmô mî yaʿamôd : " Before his indignation who can stand? " To restore the acrostic, critics generally juggle with this colon, bringing *zaʿmô* to the beginning of the verse. This move entails the alteration of *lipnê* to *lᵉpānāyw*, which is then transposed after *yaʿamôd*, (cf. *BH*³). The above procedure is followed by R. Tournay, who states : " Le décalage dans le texte reçu peut provenir d'harmonisation avec les parallèles (Ps. XXXVIII,4 ; CII,10 etc.) ; il supprime l'emphase poétique (*zʿmw* au début du vers) ". ([91]) The fact is, however, the text presents the reader with another excellent example of *chiasmus*. See the remarks made in the commentary on vv. 2 and 4b.

lipnê zaʿmô mî yaʿamôd, should be compared in form with Ps. 147 : 17, *lipnê qārātô mî yaʿamōd*, " Before his cold who can stand? " ; though the latter text too has suffered at the hands of the critics. Cf. *BH*³.

The parallelism of *zaʿam* with *ḥarôn ʾāp* is found in Ps. 69 : 25 ; 78 : 49, and Zeph. 3 : 8. The collocation of *zaʿam* and *ʾap* is found in Is. 10 : 5,25 ; Hab. 3 : 12 ; Lam. 2 : 6. But especially noteworthy is Jer. 4 : 26, *rāʾîtî wᵉhinnēh hakkarmel hammidbār wᵉkol ʿārāyw nittᵉṣû mippᵉnê yahweh mippᵉnê ḥarôn ʾappô*, " I looked — and behold, the tilled land was desert. Its cities all lying in ruins/Before Yahweh, Before his fierce anger ", ([92]) which also throws light on the interpretation of *wᵉhaṣṣūrîm nittᵉṣû mimmennû* of Nah. 1 : 6b, the next colon but one. For in that colon, *nittᵉṣû* is frequently emended to *niṣṣᵉtû*, " are ignited " (so *BH*³) from *yṣt*, " burn kindle ". The *NEB* has " melt ". But the " pouring out " of Yahweh's wrath " like fire ", not only " burns " the rocks but causes them to " break up " also. The devastating power of Yahweh's wrath as fire is well portrayed in the Song of Moses, Deut. 32 : 22, *kî ʾēš qādᵉḥāh bᵉʾappî wattîqad ʿad šᵉʾôl taḥtît wattōʾkal ʾereṣ wîbūlāh wattᵉlahēṭ môsᵉdê hārîm*, " For fire is kindled by my anger and it burns to the depths of Sheol, devours the earth and its increase, and sets on fire the foundations of the mountains ".

ḥamātô nittᵉkāh kāʾēš : " His wrath pours out like fire ". Or " His wrath is poured out like fire ". The *NEB*'s " like a stream of fire ", is an expansion of the text. For the combination of *ntk* and *ḥmh* in reference to the pouring out of Yahweh's anger, cf. Jer. 7 :

([91]) *RB* 65 (1958) 331.
([92]) Trans. of Bright, *Jeremiah*, p. 31.

20 ; 42 : 18 ; 44 : 6 ; 2 Chron. 12 : 7 ; 34 : 21,25. The cognate phrase is found in Panammū I, *KAI*, 214 : 23, *whdd ḥr' lytkh*, " May Hadad pour out wrath upon him ". The root *ntk* is found in Ugar. and Akk.

The LXX seems to have read the text badly, offering *archás* (= VL *principatus*) and therefore presumably mistook *k'š* for *r'š*. Note the repetition of *t* and *ṣ* in this verse : *ḥmtw ntkh ... whṣrym ntṣw*.

1:7

ṭôb yahweh lᵉmāʿôz : " Better is Yahweh than a fortress ". This version has been suggested by M. Dahood who takes the *lᵉ* of *lᵉmāʿôz* as a comparative *lamed*, similar in function to comparative *bᵉ* and *min*. [93] The comparative function of *lᵉ* has been discussed by Fitzmyer [94] and by Albright. [95] In Cant. 1 : 2b-3a, discussed by Albright, comparative *min* is balanced by comparative *lᵉ*.

kî ṭôbîm dōdekā miyyāyin
lᵉrêaḥ šᵉmānekā ṭôbîm

Truly thy love is sweeter than wine
It is sweeter than the scent of thy perfume. [96]

bᵉyôm ṣārāh : " on the day of siege ". For this nuance of *bᵉyôm ṣārāh*, see Ps. 20 : 2 and note Ps. 37 : 39, *bᵉʿēt ṣārāh* as proposed by Dahood. [97]

wᵉyōdēaʿ : " and he cares for ". So also the *NEB*. Besides meaning " to know ", *yādaʿ* can also signify " to care for, protect " [98]

(93) Review of G. Gerleman, *Das Hohelied*, *Biblica* 45 (1964) 288 ; *idem.*, *UHP* 30.

(94) *CBQ* 18 (1956) 10-13.

(95) In *Hebrew and Semitic Studies : Presented to Godfrey Rolles Driver*, p. 2. Cf. review of this work by R. Meyer, *OLZ* 62 (1967) col. 371.

For two new examples of comparative *lᵉ* in Exod. 1 : 9-10 and Prov. 24 : 14, cf. Dahood, *Ugarit-Forschungen* 1 (1969) 21-22.

(96) Albright's translation. Dahood, *Psalms III*, p. 181, proposes a different version based on a different division of the consonants :

kî ṭôbîm dōdekā miyyāyin
lᵉrêaḥ šamnî kī (MT *šᵉmānekā*) *ṭôbîm*
How much sweeter your love than wine,
than the scent of oil how much sweeter.

(97) *Psalms I*, p. 127.

(98) On this verse, consult D. Winton Thomas, *JJS* 1 (1948) 122-124. On *ydʿ*, *idem*, *The Text of the Revised Psalter*, p. 1. Also BDB 394a ; KB 365b.

Compare EA 60 : 30, *u šarru bēlija lu ji-da-an-ni u jipqidni ina qāt* PN *rābiṣija*, " let the king, my lord, take care of me and put me under the charge of PN my governor ". ([99]) Another rendering of *yōdēaʿ ḥōsê bô* might be, " a friend of those who take refuge in Him ", since in Ugaritic and Hebrew, *dʿt* can mean " friend ". ([100]) In *UT*, 62 : 49, *dʿt* is parallel to *ḥbr*, " colleague ".

bešeṭep ʿōbēr : " when the flood sweeps over ". An alternative version would be : " from the oncoming flood ". The meaning "from" for *be* has been established in the light of Ugaritic, Phoenician, Aramaic, and Old South Arabic. ([101])

The significance of *šeṭep ʿōbēr* is clarified by comparing Ps. 124 : 4, *ʾazay hammayim šeṭāpûnû naḥlāh ʿābōr* (MT *ʿābar*) *ʿal napšēnû*, " Then the waters would have innundated us, a torrent would have rushed over us ". Notice the parallelism of the roots *šṭp* and *ʿbr*. Consider also the following texts : Dan. 11 : 10, *wešāṭap weʿābār*, "overflowing and rushing over " ; 11 : 22, *ûzerōʿôt haššāṭōp yiššāṭepû millepānāyw*, " armies shall be utterly swamped before him " ; 11 : 26, *weḥêlô yiššāṭēp wenapelû ḥalālîm rabbîm*, " and his army shall be swamped and many shall fall down slain ". Other phrases of interest are Jer. 8 : 6 *kesûs šôṭēp bammilḥāmāh*, " Like a horse charging headlong to battle ", ([102]) and Jer. 47 : 2, *lenaḥal šôṭēp*, " an innundating torrent ".

Whether Is. 54 : 8, *šeṣep* and Heb. *šeṭep* are cognates is a moot question. ZLH 837a relates *šṭp* to Aram. *šeṭap* ; Akk. *šaṭāpu* ; Ar. *šaṭafa* ; but *šeṣep* (877b) to Ar. *šaẓifa*, " aspra fuit (manus) " ; *šaẓif*, " durus indole, vehemens ". *BH*³ recommends reading *šeṭep* for *šeṣep* in Is. 54 : 8.

A. Sperber ([103]) seems to be alone in his contention that *ʿbr* here in Nahum is a masculine equivalent of *ʿebrāh*, " wrath " ; hence " And

([99]) *CAD* [I-J] 28b.

([100]) Cf. Gordon, *UT*, Glossary, No. 1080 ; Dahood, *UHP* 61 ; *idem*, *Biblica* 45 (1964) 403 ; *idem*, *Biblica* 46 (1965) 211, for *maddaʿ*, " friend " ; van der Weiden, *Verbum Domini* 44 (1966) 44.

([101]) Cf. GB 81a-b ; F. Delitzsch, *Das Buch Hiob*, p. 145 ; Albright, *BASOR* 83 (1941) 19 n. 21 ; *idem*, *JAOS* 67 (1947) 158 n. 42 ; R. Gordis, *JQR* 48 (1957-1958) 111-112 ; O. Loretz, *BZ* 2 (1958) 289-290 ; N. M. Sarna, *JBL* 78 (1959) 310-316 ; Gordon, *UT* § 10.1 ; R. Serra, *Claretianum* 7 (1967) 295-300 ; Dahood, *PNWSP* 5, 11, 12, 39 ; *idem*, *Biblica* 44 (1963) 300-301 ; *idem*, *UHP* 27 ; *idem*, *Psalms III* especially " The Grammar of the Psalter ", pp. 391 f. There is an important bibliography by McDaniel, *Biblica* 49 (1968) 199 n. 2.

([102]) Trans. of Bright, *Jeremiah*, p. 60.

([103]) *JBL* 64 (1945) 133. Cf. also Sperber's *A Historical Grammar of Biblical Hebrew* p. 658.

with a flood of wrath ". (104) The military sense of *'br* is found in Nah. 1 : 12 and 2 : 1. The likening of a conqueror or an aggressor to a flood is frequent in Near Eastern literatures and D. R. Hillers(105) has indicated the possible Akkadian and Egyptian inspiration for the Old Testament descriptions. But the same scholar has noted that Old Testament flood-imagery must often derive from the mythological combat between the god and the primeval waters.

The *NEB*, unable to come to grips with this whole verse, inserts two phrases in the text (one on the basis of the LXX), and proposes the following version :

> The Lord is a sure refuge
> for those who look to him in time of distress ;
> he cares for all who seek his protection
> and brings them safely through the sweeping flood.

1:8

kālāh ya'ᵃśeh : " He will make an end ". For the phrase *kālāh 'āśāh* with Yahweh as agent, cf. Is. 10 : 23 ; Jer. 4 : 27 ; 5 : 18 ; 30 : 11 ; 46 : 28 ; Ezek. 11 : 13 ; 20 : 17 ; Zeph. 1 : 18 ; Neh. 9 : 31. Compare Ugar. *kly*, " destroy ", in *UT*, 67 : I : 1-3, *ktmḫṣ ltn bṯn brḥ tkly bṯn 'qltn šlyṭ d šb't rašm*, " If you smite Lotan, the fleeing serpent, destroy the writhing serpent Shalyat of the seven heads ". (106)

miqqômēhû ... wᵉ'ōyᵉbāyw : " his assailants ... and his foes ". In view of the parallelism found in Ps. 59 : 2, *haṣṣîlēnî mē'ōyᵉbay 'ᵉlōhîm mitqômᵉmay* (MT *'ᵉlōhāy mimmitqômᵉmay*) *tᵉśaggᵉbēnî*, " Rescue me, God, from my foes, against my attackers be my bulwark ", (107) and *UT*, 76 : II : 24-25, *nṭ'n barṣ iby wb'pr qm aḫk*, " We have planted my foes in the nether world, and the attackers of your brother in the mud ", (108) it seems likely that consonantal *mqwmh* signifies " hostility " or " enemies ". On the basis of the LXX *tous epegeiroménous*, scholars have suggested *bᵉqāmāyw* (cf. *BH*³). W. F. Albright (109) regards such an alteration of the consonantal text as unnecessary and reads *miqqāmēhû*. An even better reading would be *miqqômēhû*, with

(104) *Idem*, *JBL* 64 (1945) 133.
(105) *Treaty-Curses and the Old Testament Prophets*, pp. 70-71.
(106) Compare Is. 27 : 1.
(107) For this version, cf. Dahood, *Psalms II*, p. 65, and for the analysis of the text, p. 67.
(108) *Ibid.*, p. 67.
(109) *CBQ* 7 (1945) 23.

min + a Phoen. form of the Qal participle plural + 3rd masc. sing. pron. suff., with *â* > *ô*. (Cf. *ʿôz* in Prov. 24 : 5 and Eccles. 8 : 1) [110]. G. R. Driver [111] defines *mqwmh* as " opposition ", and equates it with some Arabic nouns like *qawmat*^{un}, " revolt ", *maqām*^{un}, "combat", *maqāwamat*^{un}, " resistance ". (Driver does not give any references to his sources for these Arabic words !)

y^{e}*raddep ḥōšek :* " he will pursue into Darkness ". This version is open to question from the point of view of syntax. For it is not clear that the verb *rādap* can take a double accusative with the valence of transferring from one place or position to another (factitive or causative motion). Context brings out the semantic valence of transfer inherent in verbs like *śîm* (Gen. 31 : 21) ; *nātan* (Josh. 6 : 24), *nś'* (Ps. 134 : 2). However it does not seem too great an obstacle to interpreting *ḥōšek* here as either accusative of place or perhaps accusative of direction. *ḥōšek* would then clearly mean Sheol. Compare Ps. 35 : 6, *y*^{e}*hî darkām ḥōšek waḥ*^{a}*laqlaqqōt ûmal'ak yahweh rōd*^{e}*pām*, " Let their destiny be Darkness and Destruction, with the angel of Yahweh pursuing them ". [112] The parallelism of *ḥōšek* and *š*^{e}*'ôl* is noteworthy in Job 17 : 13, *'im '*^{a}*qawweh š*^{e}*'ôl bêtî baḥōšek rippadtî y*^{e}*ṣûʿāy*, " If I await Sheol as my home, / Spread my couch in Darkness ". [113] Ps. 88 has some very instructive verses :

7 *šattanî b*^{e}*bôr taḥtiyyôt*
b^{e}*maḥ*^{a}*šakkîm bim*^{e}*ṣōlôt*
You have plunged me into the lowest Pit,
into the regions dark and deep. [114]

12-13 *hay*^{e}*suppar baqqeber ḥasdekā*
'^{e}*mûnāt*^{e}*kā bā'*^{a}*baddôn*
h^{a}*yiwwādaʿ baḥōšek pil'ekā*
w^{e}*ṣidqāt*^{e}*kā b*^{e}*'ereṣ n*^{e}*šiyyāh*
Is your kindness declared in the Grave,
your fidelity in Abaddon?

[110] Consult Dahood, *Biblica* 44 (1963) 299.

[111] *JTS* 36 (1935) 300-301. Haldar, *Studies*, p. 27, follows Driver. A similar approach to the problem is that of H. J. van Dijk, *Ezekiel's Prophecy*, p. 19, who takes *mqwmh* as *māqôm* + 3 masc. sing. suffix *-ōh* ; hence *m*^{e}*qômōh*, " his enemies ", *m*^{e}*qômōh* being an abstract noun with concrete meaning.

[112] For this translation cf. Dahood, *Psalms I*, p. 208 and Commentary, p. 211.

[113] Trans. of Pope, *Job*, p. 119.

[114] Trans. of Dahood, *Psalms II*, p. 301.

Are your marvels made known in the Darkness,
Your generosity in the land of forgetfulness? (115)

Cf. further, 1 Sam. 2 : 9 ; Job 10 : 21 ; 18 : 18 ; 20 : 26 ; Eccles. 11 : 8. For references to Yahweh pursuing his enemies, cf. Is. 41 : 3 ; Jer 2 : 18 ; Ps. 83 : 16 ; Lam. 3 : 43,66.

The syllable count in this verse is 9/9 with a 3/3 stress count. The verse contains yet another example of *chiasmus.*

1:9

mah teḥaššebûn 'el yahweh : " Why do you plot against Yahweh? " The verb *ḥšb* is found with three prepositions : *'el* (cf. also Hos. 7 : 15) ; *'al* (cf. v. 11 below) and *le* (e.g. Ps. 41 : 8). The interchange of these prepositions is similar to that found in Ugaritic between *'l* and *l.* (116)

lō' tāqûm pa'amayim ṣārāh : " his adversaries will not rise up twice ". W. F. Albright (117) sees this colon as a perfect parallel to the first colon of v. 8, *kālāh ya'aśeh miqqômēhû,* and believes that both cola formed part of a more complex original. Albrights' vocalisation *ṣārêhū* need not be followed, since *ṣārāh* can now be shown to be an abstract noun with a concrete meaning as in *UT*, 68 : 9, *ht ibk tmḫṣ ht tṣmt ṣrtk,* " Now you will smite your foe, now you will overthrow your adversary ". Similarly, in 'nt : IV : 48, *mnm ib yp' lb'l ṣrt lrkb 'rpt,* " What foe has risen against Baal, what enemy against the Rider of the Clouds ". (118) Cf. Exod. 23 : 22 ; Ps. 54 : 9 (*ṣārāh* = " my adversaries " balancing *'ōyebay,* " my enemies ") and Ps. 138 : 7. A. Haldar (119) has already recognized this usage. Most recently, T. H. Gaster has clung to the general belief that in this Nahumic text, *ṣārāh* has the notion of " rebellion " or " opposition ". (120) Correctly, the *NEB* has " adversaries ". In the light of the evidence presented above, one can no longer accept J. M. P. Smith's comment that " MT's thought is too abstract and colourless for the context".(121)

(115) *Ibid.*, p. 302.

(116) Cf. *UT*, pp. 99 f., § 10.13, for remarks on *UT*, 51 : VIII : 5-6 ; Dahood, *UHP* 31 ; *idem, Psalms I*, p. 250.

(117) *CBQ* 7 (1945) 23.

(118) Cf. van der Weiden, *Verbum Domini* 44 (1966) 43-52 ; Dahood, *UHP* 44 ; *idem, Psalms I*, pp. 32 f. ; and note *UT*, Glossary No. 2200, *ṣrt,* " enemy ".

(119) *Studies*, p. 31.

(120) *Myth, Legend, and Custom* p. 665. For an earlier definition of *ṣārāh* on the basis of Akk. *ṣarrātu,* " hostilities ", cf. Driver, *JTS* 39 (1938) 269.

(121) *CECBN* 293. On the basis of LXX *ekdikēsei,* Smith reads *yiqqôm,* " take vengeance ", for MT *tāqûm* (p. 301).

The emendations found in the apparatus of *BH*³ (*yāqûmû ... ṣārāyw*) can also be ignored.

The Ugaritic texts have made it possible for us to distinguish between Heb. *ṣārāh*, " siege ; distress " (as in v. 7) and Heb. *ṣārāh*, " adversary, enemy ; hostility " :

a) Heb. *ṣrr*, " show hostility towards " etc.,
ṣārāh, " adversary, enemy ; hostility ".
Ugar. *ṣrr*, " hurt " etc. ;
ṣrt, " hostility ; enemy ".
b) Heb. *ṣwr*, " besiege ".
Ugar. *ṣwr*, " besiege ".

paʿᵃmayim : " twice ". Heb. *paʿam* ; Phoen. *pʿm* ; but Ugar. *pʿn*. C. H. Gordon believes that Heb. *paʿam* is a blend of *pʿm*, " time " and *pʿn*, " foot ", with both meanings. [122] E. Y. Kutscher [123] observes however that *paʿam* is probably like Heb. *regel*, which can mean both " foot " and " time ". Regarding Aistleitner's listing of Akk. *pēnu* and *pēmu*, [124] it should be noted that *pēmu* is the normal base form and that *pēn-* only occurs before suffixes (*penšu* etc.). The writing of the *m* as *n* before suffixes is not in itself warrant to speak of a base *pēn-*, since this is a normal phonologically conditioned change which does not imply an alloform independent base. This does not rule out a secondary base form however, and in fact von Soden lists a writing *pè-nu* from Ugarit. [125] It remains to be seen if a form *pēnu* is limited to texts in the West Semitic area.

1 : 10

This must be one of the most difficult texts in the Old Testament. No satisfactory translation of the passage has been offered to date. A recent attempt is that of S. J. de Vries, who " produces " the following Heb. text and English translation : *kî ʿad sîrîm sᵉbūkîm ûkᵉsōbᵉbîm sᵉbūkîm ʾukkᵉlû kᵉqaš yābēš mālēʾ*, " for it will be like interlacing thorns and as intertwining brambles, devoured like completely dried-out chaff ". [126] Unfortunately he has no philological commentary to explain his results.

(122) *UT*, Glossary No. 1998.
(123) *JSS* 10 (1965) 23.
(124) *WuS* 2243.
(125) *AHw* 854 and ref. there to *Ugaritica V*, 239, 18. I am grateful to R. Caplice for observations on this whole question.
(126) S. J. de Vries, *VT* 16 (1966) 476-481, esp. 480.

kî ʿōd : " For again ". The MT has *kî ʿad.*

sîrîm s^ebūkîm : " entangled thorns ". The root *sbk* is not common and the verb only occurs once elsewhere, viz. Job 8 : 17. The noun *s^ebak* means a " thicket " in Gen. 22 : 13 ; Is. 9 : 17 ; 10 : 34.

ûk^esōb^eʾīm s^ebûʾîm : " and like drunkards sodden with drink ". A dubious version, but the MT, *ûk^esobʾām s^ebûʾîm,* is quite problematical. J. Reider has suggested that the first *mēm* is enclitic and obtains the translation " and as the drunken are getting drunk ".(127) *sbʾ* means " drink " as is clear from Prov. 23 : 20, *ʾal t^ehî b^esōb^eʾê yāyin b^ezōl^alê bāśār lāmô,* " Be not among winebibbers, or among gluttonous eaters of meat ". Cf. also Deut. 21 : 20 ; Is. 1 : 22 ; 56 : 12. The Akkadian cognate is *sābû/sābî.* Akk. *sābītum* means a " woman-publican " in charge of an alehouse or tavern. (128) In the Mari texts there is reference to the *bītāt sabī,* " taverns ". (129) A. Haldar's equation of Heb. *sbʾ* with Ugar. *spʾ,* " eat ", (130) is interesting but questionable, since Heb. *mispôʾ,* " fodder " is related to Ugar. *spʾ.* Haldar also relates *sîrîm* to an Akk. word *sīru* which he claims means " mesh (of a net) ", (131) but he gives no evidence and the present writer has not found any either. Both Haldar's philological analysis and his translation are strange : " For into the very meshes are they interwoven, and as they consume a consuming, they are eaten as chaff wholly dry ". (132)

ʾukk^elû k^eqaš yābēš mālē : " They will be consumed like very dry chaff ". The idea of the consumption of the enemy like chaff or stubble in a fire should be easy to understand in the light of texts like Exod. 15 : 7, *ûb^erōb g^eʾôn^ekā tah^arōs qāmekā t^ešallaḥ ḥ^arōn^ekā yōʾk^elēmô kaqqaš,* " In the greatness of your majesty you overthrew your adversaries, you sent forth your fury, it consumed them like stubble ". Note the collocation of stubble, chaff and thorns in Is. 33 : 11-12, *tah^arû ḥ^ašaš tēl^edû qaš rûḥī k^emō* (MT *rûḥ^akem*) *ʾēš tōʾkalkem, w^ehāyû ʿammîm miśr^epôt śîd qôṣîm k^esûḥîm bāʾēš yiṣṣattû,* " You will

(127) *JJS* 3 (1952) 79.

(128) Cf. Driver and Miles, *The Babylonian Laws,* II, p. 197 (commentary) ; p. 396 (Glossary) ; R. Borger, *Babylonisch-assyrische Lesestücke* I, Glossar, p. LXXVI.

(129) Cf. M. Birot, *Textes administratifs de la salle 5 du palais,* p. 27, text 27 IV 15.

(130) *Studies,* p. 32.

(131) *Ibid.*

(132) *Ibid.,* p. 81.

conceive chaff, you will bring forth stubble; my breath like fire will consume you. And the peoples will be as if burned with lime, like thorns cut down, that are burned in the fire". Cf. also Is. 47 : 14.

The connection of "drunkards" with "thorns" and "stubble" is difficult to explain, though the above texts do give a clearer picture in conjunction with Obad. 16-18, where "drunkenness" is followed by the "burning" of the faithless and worthless "house of Esau" (v.18).

'ukkᵉlû should be repointed perhaps to *'ūkᵉlû*, passive *qal.* (133) *ml'* has been taken here as an adverb with a function similar to that of *mᵉ'ōd.* See the commentary on Nah. 2 : 2 for the adjectival and adverbial role of *m'd* in Heb. and Ugar.

Although one must not underestimate the size of the problems in this verse, there is one point which must not be overlooked, namely, the function of the particle *kî.* J. Muilenburg (134) has stressed how this particle plays an important role in Hebrew poetry and how it appears at strategic points. In the context here, the *kî* of v. 10 seems to indicate that the introductory poem or hymn has reached its conclusion, for the next verse (11) is directly addressed to Nineveh, whereas the previous verses have referred in a more general way to the enemies of Yahweh (though of course the Assyrians would be the foremost in mind).

1:11

mimmēk : "From you". Clearly Nineveh is being addressed here directly for the first time. In v. 9 a question is delivered to the enemies of Yahweh generally. That verse is part of the introductory hymn or psalm. V. 11, however, is more specifically addressed to Nineveh, and although it does not constitute part of the psalm which ends in vv. 9-10, nevertheless there is a cleverly constructed link between v. 11 and v. 9. Thus the verb *ḥšb* plays a vital role: *mah tᵉḥaššᵉbûn 'el yahweh* (v. 9); *ḥōšēb ʿal yahweh rāʿāh* (v. 11). Notice the similar repetition of a phrase in vv. 8-9 *kālāh yaʿᵃśeh* (v. 8); *kālāh hû' ʿōśeh* (v. 9).

ḥōšēb ʿal yahweh rāʿāh : "one who plots evil against Yahweh". For the preposition in the phrase *ḥōšēb ʿal*, cf. commentary on v. 9 above.

yōʿēṣ bᵉliyyāʿal : "one who is a counsellor of Belial". The most convincing proposal for the etymology of *bᵉliyyaʿal* is that made by

(133) *'ukkᵉlû* is regarded as a passive qal by R. J. Williams, in *Essays on the Ancient Semitic World*, p. 46.

(134) *JBL* 88 (1969) 13-14.

D. Winton Thomas, [135] who derives it from *blʿ*, " swallow ". Note the repetition of ʿ in *ʿal yahweh rāʿāh yōʿēṣ bᵉliyyāʿal*.

1:12

kōh 'āmar yahweh : " Thus says Yahweh ". Compare this with Mari *kī'am iqbi(m)*, " thus he spoke ". [136]

'im šᵉlēmîm wᵉkēn rabbîm : " Even though they are strong and many ". This is a doubtful rendering of a very difficult phrase. The LXX *katárchōn hudátōn pollōn* clearly represents a different division of the consonants, perhaps *mōšēl mayim rabbîm* (so *BH*³) or *hammōšᵉlîm mayim rabbîm* (J. Gray) [137]. The most recent adherent of the *mayim rabbîm* is T. H. Gaster, who reads : *'im šālū mayim rabbîm*, [138] " What though whole oceans gushed " ! [139] To support our interpretation of *šᵉlēmîm* as " strong ", with the sense of " hale, healthy ", we compare the meaning of *šlm* in *UT*, 1019 : 2-6, *ilm tǵrk tšlmk tʿzzk alp ymm wrbt šnt bʿd ʿlm*, " May the gods protect you, keep you hale, strengthen you, for a thousand days, ten thousand years, so long as eternity perdures ". [140]

wᵉnāgōzzû wᵉʿubbᵉrû : " they will be cut down and overwhelmed ". The MT reads : *wᵉkēn nāgōzzû wᵉʿābār w ...* One could read *wᵉʿūbᵉrû*, qal passive. *ʿbr*, " overwhelm " has been discussed in the commentary on *šeṭep ʿōbēr*, in v. 8. Heb. *gzz*, is cognate to Ugar. *gzz*, " to shear ".

ʿinnītīk lō' 'aʿannēk ʿôd, " I have oppressed you, but I will not oppress you again ". *ʿnh*, " oppress ", is found in Moabite Mesha, *KAI*, 181:5-6, *ʿmry mlk yśr'l wyʿnw 't m'b ymn rbn ky y'np kmš b'rṣh wyḥlph bnh wy'mr gm h' "nw 't m'b*, " Omri, king of Israel, he oppressed Moab many days, for Chemosh was angry with his land. And

[135] " *bᵉliyyaʿal* in the Old Testament ", in *Biblical and Patristic Studies in Memory of Robert Pierce Casey*, pp. 11-19. Cf. also, F. M. Cross and D. N. Freedman, *JBL* 72 (1953) 22 n. 6 ; Dahood, *Psalms I*, p. 105 ; *HALAT* 128. Most recently, N. J. Tromp, *Primitive Conceptions*, pp. 125-128.

[136] See now the excellent article by W. L. Moran, " New Evidence from Mari on the History of Prophecy ", *Biblica* 50 (1969) 15-56, esp. 24-26, where introductory formulae are discussed.

[137] *VT* 6 (1956) 280 ; cf. also, *idem*, *VT* 11 (1961) 17.

[138] *Myth, Legend, and Custom*, p. 727. *šālū* is derived by Gaster from Akk. and Ar.

[139] *Ibid.*, p. 666.

[140] Trans. of Dahood, *Psalms III*, p. 282.

his son succeeded him and he too said, ' I will oppress Moab' ". [141] *'nh* occurs several times in Phoen. Karatepe, *KAI*, 26 : AI : 18-20. There is some discussion as to the meaning of Ugar. *'ny* in *UT*, 137 : 28, *wank 'ny mlak ym t'dt ṯpṭ nhr*, " And I'll answer the messengers of Yamm, The envoys of Judge Nahar " (Ginsberg, *ANET* 130). Like Ginsberg, C. H. Gordon takes *'ny/w* to mean " answer ", though in fact Ginsberg thinks " humble " is also possible. [142] M. Held opts for the rendering " humble ". [143]

The *scriptio defectiva* in *'innītīk* (*'ntk*) is interesting but not necessarily useful in a discussion of the date of the passage here. According to Albright, [144] Cross and Freedman, [145] medial *matres lectionis* were introduced into Biblical Hebrew under the influence of Aramaic about the 6th cent. B.C. However, recent epigraphical discoveries in Israel may require a new appraisal of the situation. [146]

1 : 13

wᵉ'attāh : " And now. " On the particle (*wᵉ*)*'attāh* for rhetorical analysis, cf. J. Muilenburg, *JBL* 88 (1969) 15.

'ešbōr mōṭēhû : " I will break his yoke ". There is no reason for emending MT *mōṭēhû*, " his yoke ", to *maṭṭēhû*, " his sceptre " (*BH*³). True, in Is. 14 : 5 and Jer. 48 : 17, there is a collocation of *šbr* and *maṭṭeh*, but *šbr* is found with *môṭāh* in Jer. 28 : 10-12 ; and Lev. 26 : 13, *wᵉ'ešbōr mōṭōt 'ullᵉkem*, " and I have broken the bars of your yoke ". Likewise in Ezek. 30 : 18, *bᵉšibrî šām 'et mōṭôt miṣrayim*, " when I break there the yoke of Egypt " there is no necessity for emending (following the versions, cf. *BH*³) *mōṭôt* to *maṭṭôt* or *maṭṭeh*. [147] Furthermore, the parallelism of *mōṭēhû* and *môsᵉrōtayik* is matched by the collocation in Jer. 27 : 2, *môsērôt ûmōṭôt*. The *môṭ* or *môṭāh* is, strictly speaking, the " bar " of the " yoke ", rather than the whole " yoke ", but one can take *môṭ* here *pars pro toto*. [148]

[141] Trans. of Ullendorff, in *Documents from Old Testament Times*, edited by D. Winton Thomas, p. 196.

[142] *ANET* 130, footnote.

[143] *Eretz-Israel* 9 (1969) 72 n. 15.

[144] *JBL* 51 (1932) 81.

[145] *Early Hebrew Orthography*, p. 57.

[146] Cf. Y. Aharoni, *BASOR* 197 (1970) 21.

[147] Cf. GB 404b ; ZLH 416b ; KB 503b ; *HALAT* 73b.

[148] It is hardly an objection when G. G. V. Stonehouse, *The Books of the Prophets Zephaniah and Nahum*, p 111, argues that *môṭ* is used in the sense of " pole " but not in the sense of " yoke ".

ûmôs^erōtayik 'anattēq : " and your bonds I will snap ". Or perhaps " and your bonds I will pull (tear) off ". For the collocation of *ntq* and *môsērôt*, cf. Jer. 2 : 20 ; 5 : 5 ; 30 : 8 ; Ps. 2 : 3 ; 107 : 14. (149) In Judg. 16 : 9,12 *ntq* is used with *hay^etārîm*, " cords ". Lexicographers universally derive *môsērôt* from the root *'sr*. But it may well be derived from *ysr*, " instruct, chasten ". (150)

The verse is chiastic, with an 8 : 4 : 9 syllable count, *mē'ālāyik* serving as a double-duty modifier. (151)

1 : 14

w^eṣiwwāh 'ālekā yahweh : " And Yahweh commands thus concerning you ". For Yahweh commanding, cf. Is. 23 : 11 ; 34 : 16 ; Jer. 47 : 7 ; Ezek. 37 : 10, and note the variety of prepositions used with *ṣwh*.

The masc. suffixes indicate that Yahweh is commanding the king of Nineveh.

lō' yizzāra'-m šim^ekā 'ôd : " Your name shall not be sown again ". The MT reads : *lō yizzāra' miššim^ekā 'ôd* (cf. LXX *ou sparēsetai ek tou onómatós sou*). The *mi-* of MT *miššim^ekā* is strange and one should probably read the *m* as enclitic after *yizzāra'*. This has already been proposed by A. Haldar, (152) but has not as yet received attention from critics. The existence of enclitic *mēm* in Hebrew is now even more clearly established. The major study of H. Hummel (153) has given an impetus to further research and more examples are turning up. Even if subsequent research turns up a different explanation for the *m-* of our verse, there is no justification for the emendation proposed by *BH*³ (to read *yizzākēr* for *yizzāra'*), but recently adopted by J. Jeremias. (154) The following will show that the text is sound.

šēm, literally " name ", here refers to " posterity, progeny, memory "; Akk. *šumu* = " name ", but also " son ". (155) Such progeny

(149) Notice also the parallelism of *šbr* // *ntq* in Jer 2 : 20 ; 5 : 5 ; 30 : 8. Jer 30 : 8 *mē'al* compares with *mē'ālāyik* in our verse in Nahum.

(150) Cf. *UT*, Glossary No. 1120 ; Dahood, *Psalms I*, p. 59.

(151) On this term, and for examples of the phenomenon, cf. Dahood, *CBQ* 29 (1967) 574-579.

(152) *Studies*, p. 36.

(153) *JBL* 76 (1957) 85-107.

(154) *Kultprophetie und Gerichtsverkündigung*, p. 21.

(155) Cf. J. J. Stamm, *Die akkadische Namengebung*, pp. 40-42 ; Haldar, *Studies*, p. 36 ; R. T. O'Callaghan, *VT* 4 (1954) 164-165 ; Pope, *Job*, p. 38 ; Dahood, *Psalms I*, p. 250.

would have carried on the power of his father. Note the collocation in Is. 66 : 22, *kēn yaʿamōd zarʿakem wešimkem,* " So shall your descendants and your name remain " (*RSV*) ; also Is. 56 : 5, *wenātattî lāhem bebêtî ûbeḥômōtay yād wāšēm ṭôb mibbānîm ûmibbānôt,* " I will give them in my house and within my walls a memorial and a name better than sons and daughters ", (J. L. McKenzie). ([156]) Note Is. 14 : 22 (*šēm* = " posterity ", parallel to *nîn,* " offspring ") ; 48 : 19 ; 2 Sam. 14 : 7 ; Ps. 9 : 6 ; Job 18 : 17 ; Prov. 10 : 7,11. The collocation of *zeraʿ* and *šēm* in Is. 66 : 22 is matched in Aramaic Nêrab, *KAI,* 225 : 9-11, *šhr wšmš wnkl wnšk ysḥw šmk wʾšrk mn ḥyn wmwt lḥh ykṭlwk wyhʾbdw zrʿk,* " May *ŠHR* and *ŠMŠ* and *NKL* and *NŠK* tear out your name and your house from the living ! And with an evil death may they kill you and cause your seed to perish ", ([157]) and in Aram. Têmā, *KAI,* 228 : 13-14, *ʾlhy tymʾ ynsḥwhy wzrʿh wšmh mn ʾnpy tymʾ,* " May the gods of Tema uproot him and his posterity and his name from Tema ". Noteworthy is the combination of *ʾšm* and *qbr* in *AIS,* II : A : 4, [*wʾšmh y*]*tnšy wyhwh qb*[*rh*], " [and may his name be for]gotten, and may [his grav]e be ... ". ([158]) Precisely *šmk* and *qbrk* are found in Nah. 1 : 14.

mibbêt ʾelōhekā : " From your temple ". Compare Ugar. *bt il,* " temple " (*UT,* 14 : 1 ; 2100 : 15) ; *bt ilm rbm,* " Temple of the Great Gods " (*UT,* 1090 : 1-2) ; Phoen.-Punic *bt ʾlm* ; Akk. *bīt ili,* " temple ".

ʾakrît : " I will cut off ". A literal translation. Compare Zech. 13 : 2, *ʾakrît ʾet šemôt hāʿaṣabbîm min hāʾāreṣ,* " I will cut off the names of the idols from the land " (*RSV*), i.e. " destroy the memory of " etc.

pesel ûmassēkāh : " the carved and molten image(s) ". The Heb. nouns are in the singular, but one could render them by English plurals. The pair *pesel/massēkāh* is common ; cf. Deut. 27 : 15 ; Judg. 17 : 3,4 ; 18 : 14,17,18 ; Is. 30 : 22 ; 42 : 17 ; Hab. 2 : 18 ; 2 Chron. 34 : 3,4. Note also Is. 48 : 5, *ûpislî weniskî,* " my carved image and my molten image ". Although translators frequently define *pesel* as " carved image " and *massēkāh* as " molten image ", the distinction between the two is not easily made. Is. 40 : 19, *happesel nāsak ḥārāš,* " the craftsman casts the image ", and Is. 44 : 10, *mî yāṣar ʾēl ûpesel nāsāk,* " who fashions a god or casts an image ", show that *pesel* is

([156]) *Second Isaiah,* p. 149.

([157]) This English version follows closely the German of H. Donner and W. Röllig, *KAI,* II, p. 275. For a slightly different version, cf. the trans. of S. Gevirtz, *VT* 11 (1961) 148.

([158]) As rendered by Fitzmyer, *AIS,* pp. 80-81.

not necessarily " carved " or " sculptured ". C. H. Gordon ([159]) notes that Ugar. *psl* has a broader meaning than " sculptor ". M. Dahood ([160]) has noted that before the discovery of the Ras Shamra texts, the root *psl* appeared only in Heb. and Aram. Phoen. *mskt* occurs in the Karatepe Inscription, where the king relates that he offered sacrifices *lkl hmskt*, " to all the molten images " (*KAI*, 26 : AIII : 1).

1:14

'aššîm qibrekā : " I will devastate your grave ". Instead of MT *'āśîm*, read *'aššîm*, hiph. imperf. of *šmm*, as suggested by a number of scholars — Sellin, Horst, Delcor, and Gaster. Cf. KB 989a *sub voce šmm.* Perhaps literally *'aššîm* means " I will cause your grave to be made desolate ". Just as there was fear of the threat of no burial — a threat common in the treaty-curses of the Ancient Near East and examined by D. R. Hillers ([161]) in the prophetical books of the Old Testament, so also there must have been dread of the destruction of the grave.

An alternative would be to retain MT *'āśîm* and render it : " I will determine " or perhaps " I will mark out ". G. Leonardi ([162]) has suggested that Heb. *śym*, Ugar. *šyt* could have this meaning.

kî qallôtā : " because you are worthless ". Some critics prefer a noun to a verb and emend *qlwt* to *qlwn* (cf. *BH*³). G. R. Driver on the other hand proposed long ago the existence of a noun *qlyt*, which he described however as an " abstract with semi-concrete meaning "([163]) and he rendered the whole colon : " I will make thy grave as (a thing of) shame ". ([164]) A. Haldar would relate *qallôtā* to Ugar *qll*, " fall " ; hence " thou hast fallen ". ([165]) Certainly this possibility has to be considered.

([159]) *UT*, Glossary No. 2073.

([160]) *Psalms II*, p. 246.

([161]) *Treaty-Curses and the Old Testament Prophets* pp. 68-69. Cf. also our comments on Nah. 3 : 19.

([162]) *Biblica* 49 (1968) 240-241.

([163]) *JTS* 39 (1938) 270.

([164]) *Ibid.*

([165]) *Studies*, p. 38. For Ugar. *qll*, " fall, cf. *UT*, Glossary No. 2231 ; *WuS* 2408 ; M. Held, *Eretz Israel* 9 (1969) 74 n. 32, (Ugar. *qll* = Heb. *npl*). The root could be *qw/yl.* Cf. W. von Soden, VTS 16 (1967) 295 (= Akk. *qālu*, " fall ") ; J. C. de Moor, *Ugarit-Forschungen* 1 (1969) 173.

2:1

hinnēh ... mašmîaʿ šālôm : " Behold ... announces peace ". Similar language is found in Deutero-Isaiah. Cf. Is. 52 : 7. In fact, J. Gray maintains that Deutero-Isaiah is merely re-echoing Nahum. ([166])

mᵉbaśśēr : " brings good tidings ". That the tidings are good is clear from the context in which *bśr* is used here. But *bśr* does not always imply the notion of good tidings. Cf. 1 Sam 4 : 17 f., where the *mᵉbaśśēr* gives news bad enough to cause Eli to fall off his seat and break his neck. A. L. Oppenheim ([167]), in a review of published texts from Mari, strongly opposes the translation of Akk. *bussurum* by " to convey good news ". For him *bussurum* means simply " to bring a message ", and *bus(s)urtu,* " message ". But note that *CAD* [B] 347 f., lists : *bussuru,* 1. " to praise, extol " ; 2. " to report, to bring news pleasant to the listener " ; 346 lists *bussurtu,* " unexpected tidings (usually good) " ; *busāru,* " announcement ". The root *bšr* occurs a number of times in Ugaritic. E.g., *UT,* 51 : V : 88-89, *tbšr bʿl bšrtk yblt,* " Receive, Baal, the glad tidings I bring thee " (Ginsberg, *ANET* 133). The root has been studied by D. J. McCarthy, who translates the above Ugar. text thus : " Evangelizare, Baal, evangelium tibi apportatur ". ([168])

mašmîaʿ šālôm : " of one who announces peace ! " With *mašmîaʿ šālôm,* compare Lachish, *yšmʿ yhwh ʾt ʾdny šmʿt šlm,* " May Yahweh make my lord hear of peace ". ([169])

ḥoggî yᵉhûdāh ḥaggayik : " Celebrate your feasts, O Judah ! " G. Ryckmans ([170]) suggests that the primitive sense of *ḥgg* and *ḥwg* is " se rendre à une fête, faire un pèlerinage ", and that " entourer, faire le tour de ", is only a secondary sense. W. A. Ward ([171]) compares Heb. *ḥāgag,* " celebrate a feast ", with Egyptian *ḥʾg,* " be glad, joyous ".

([166]) *VT* 11 (1961) 17,21.
([167]) *JNES* 13 (1954) 145.
([168]) " Vox *bśr* praeparat vocem ' evangelium ' ", *Verbum Domini* 42 (1964) 26-33, this text, 28. Note also R. Dussaud, *RHR* 3 (1935) 21 " Rejois-toi (ô) Baʿal ! " ; Dahood, *Psalms II,* p. 141, who renders *tbšr,* " Rejoice ".
([169]) Cf. *DISO* 310.
([170]) *Muséon* 78 (1965) 468. Cf. *HALAT* 278.
([171]) *Orientalia* 31 (1962) 405 n. 6.

šallᵉmî nᵉdārāyik : " Fulfill your vows ". A common biblical expression; cf. Ps. 22 : 26. Compare Neo-Punic Hofra, *šlmty 't ndry*, ([172]) " I have fulfilled my vow ".

kullōh nikrāt : " he has been wholly destroyed ". *kullōh* is *kōl* plus 3rd masc. sing. suffix. Cf. GK, p. 256e. The LXX, *syntetélestai* seems to be based on an interpretation of *klh* as some form of the verb *kālāh*.

([172]) Cf. *DISO* 303 for list of references (*sub šlm*).

Chapter II

Nahum 2 : 2-14

Text: Nahum 2:2-4

Syllable Count	Stress Count		
8	3	עִלה מֵפִיץ עַל־פִּנַיִךְ	2
9	4	נָצוֹר מְצֻרָה צַפֵּה־דֶרֶךְ	
5	2	חַזֵּק מָתְנַיִם	
5	3	אַמֵּץ כֹּחַ מְאֹד	
10	4	כִּי שִׁב יַהְוֶה אֶת־גְּאוֹן יַעֲקֹב	3
6	2	כִּגְאוֹן יִשְׂרָאֵל	
7	3	כִּי בִקָקוּם בֹּקְקִים	
8	3	וּזְמֹרֵיהֶם שִׁחֵתוּ	
9	3	מָגֵן גִּבֹּרֵיהוּ מְאָדָּם	4
8	3	אַנְשֵׁי־חַיִל מְתֻלָּעִים	
8	3	בְּאֵשׁ פְּלָדוֹת הָרֶכֶב	
5	2	בְּיוֹם הֲכִינוֹ	
8	3	וְהַבְּרֹשִׁים הָרְעָלוּ	

Translation: Nahum 2 : 2-4

2 A scatterer is coming up against you;
guard your fortifications, watch the road;
Strengthen your loins,
summon all your strength.

3 For Yahweh is restoring the glory of Jacob,
like the glory of Israel;
For plunderers plundered them,
and their vines they destroyed.

4 The shields of his men are red
his warriors are dressed in scarlet;
Fiery are the caparisons of the horses
on the day of array,
and the spears are shaking.

Text: Nahum 2 : 5-8

Syllable Count	Stress Count		
7	3	בַּחוּצוֹת יִתְהוֹלְלוּ	5
3	1	הָרֶכֶב	
8	3	יִשְׁתַּקְשְׁקוּן בָּרְחֹבוֹת	
7	3	מַרְאֵיהֶן כַּלַּפִּידִם	
8	3	כַּבְּרָקִים יְרוֹצֵצוּ	
6	2	יִזְכֹּר אַדִּירָיו	6
9	3	יִכָּשְׁלוּ בַּהֲלְכוֹתָם	
7	2	יְמַהֲרוּ חוֹמָתָהּ	
6	2	וְהָכֵן הַסֹּכֵךְ	
10	3	שַׁעֲרֵי הַנְּהָרוֹת נִפְתָּחוּ	7
6	2	וְהַהֵיכָל נָמוֹג	
11	3	וְהֻצַּב גֻּלְּתָה הֹעֲלָתָה	8
9	3	וְאַמְהֹתֶיהָ מְנַהֲגוֹת	
4	2	כְּקוֹל יוֹנִים	
9	3	מְתֹפְפֹת עַל־לִבְבֵהֶן	

Translation: Nahum 2:5-8

5 Through the streets wildly race
the horses,
they rush to and fro in the squares;
their appearance like torches,
like lightning they flash by.

6 His officers are strong,
they stumble forward in their march;
they speed towards the wall,
and they set up the protector.

7 The sluice-gates of the canals are opened,
and the palace is melting;

8 The beauty has been stripped and carried off,
and her handmaids are moaning
like the sound of doves,
and they are beating upon their breasts.

Text : Nahum 2 : 9-12

Syllable Count	Stress Count	Text	Verse
9	3	וְנִינְוֵה כִבְרֵכַת־מַיִם	9
8	3	מִימֵי הִיא וְהֵמָּה נָסִים	
6	2	עִמְדוּ עֲמֹדוּ	
4	2	וְאֵין מַפְנֶה	
8	4	בֹּזּוּ כֶסֶף בֹּזּוּ זָהָב	10
8	4	וְאֵין קֵצֶה לַתְּכוּנָה	
8	4	כָּבֹד מִכֹּל כְּלִי חֶמְדָּה	
11	4	בּוּקָה וּמְבוּקָה וּמְבֻלָּקָה	11
9	4	וְלֵב נָמֵס וּפִק בִּרְכַּיִם	
9	4	וְחַלְחָלָה בְּכָל־מָתְנַיִם	
10	4	וּפְנֵי כֻלָּם קִבְּצוּ פָארוּר	
7	3	אַיֵּה מְעוֹן אֲרָיוֹת	12
9	4	וּמְעָרָה הִיא לַכְּפִרִים	
9	5	אֲשֶׁר הָלַךְ אַרְיֵה לִביא שָׁם	
8	4	גּוּר אַרְיֵה וְאֵין מַחֲרִיד	

Translation: Nahum 2 : 9-12

9 Nineveh is like a pool of water,
its waters running away ;
Stop ! Stop !
but no one turns back.

10 Plunder the silver, plunder the gold,
for there is no end to the treasure ;
an abundance of all precious things.

11 Plunder, slaughter, devastation,
melting hearts and trembling of knees ;
And there is anguish in all loins,
and the faces of all gather paleness.

12 Where is the den of the lions,
and the cave for the young lions?
Where the lion, the lioness went,
the lion's cubs and none to frighten them away.

Text: Nahum 2:13-14

Syllable Count	Stress Count		
9	4	אַרְיֵה טֹרֵף בְּדֵי גֹרוֹתָיו	13
9	4	וּמְחַנֵּק לְלִבְאֹתָיו	
8	3	וַיְמַלֵּא־טֶרֶף חֹרָיו	
8	3	וּמְעֹנֹתָיו טְרֵפָה	
		הִנְנִי אֵלַיִךְ	14
		נְאֻם יַהְוֶה צְבְאוֹת	
9	3	וְהִבְעִרְתִּי בֶעָשָׁן רִכְבָּהּ	
9	3	וּכְפִירַיִךְ תֹּאכַל חָרֶב	
9	3	וְהִכְרַתִּי מֵאֶרֶץ טַרְפֵּךְ	
11	5	וְלֹא־יִשָּׁמַע עוֹד קוֹל מַלְאָכָיִךְ	

Translation: Nahum 2 : 13-14

13 The lion tore up for the needs of his cubs,
and strangled (prey) for his lionesses;
He filled his caves with prey,
and his dens with torn flesh.

14 Behold I am against you —
Oracle of Yahweh Sabaot —
I will burn your chariots in smoke,
and the sword will devour your young lions;
I will destroy your prey from the earth,
and the voice of your messengers will be heard no more.

Philological Commentary

2 : 2

ʿālāh : " is coming up ". That is, to attack. *ʿālāh* has this sense in a number of contexts. A good example is Jer. 48 : 18, *kî šōdēd môʾāb ʿālāh bāk šiḥēt mibṣārāyik,* " For Moab's destroyer has attacked you, destroyed your strongholds ". Dahood compares Phoen. Ahiram, *KAI,* 1 : 2, *wʾl mlk bmlkm wskn bs*[*k*]*nm wtʾ mḥnt ʿly gbl,* " If any king whatever, or any governor whatever, or camp commandant should attack Byblos ". (1) A Ugaritic example is found in *UT,* 2060 : 31, *ib ʿltn,* " the enemy has come up against me ". (2)

mēpîṣ : " A scatterer ". *mēpîṣ* has frequently been emended to *mappēṣ,* " war-club, mace ", which is found along-side nine occurrences of *nippaṣtî,* " I will smash ", in Jer. 51 : 20-23. Prov. 25 : 18,

> *mēpîṣ wᵉḥereb wᵉḥēṣ šānûn*
> *ʾîš ʿōneh bᵉrēʿēhû ʿēd šāqer,*

is rendered by R. B. Y. Scott :

> Like a mace, a sword, or a sharp-pointed arrow,
> Is the man who gives false evidence against his neighbour. (3)

But there is no note to indicate whether he takes *mēpîṣ* as " mace " or whether he emends it to *mappēṣ.* The *NEB* has " battering-ram ", but there is no footnote to explain it The root of *mēpîṣ* is *pwṣ,* " to scatter, disperse ". *pûṣ* (Hiph. *hēpîṣ*) is often used in military contexts to express the idea of putting the enemy in confusion and routing them. Cf. Ps. 18 : 15 and Ps. 144 : 6, where *pwṣ* parallels *hmm,* " to throw into commotion " Another text of interest is Is 24 : 1. Cf. the commentary on Nah 2 : 3. Haldar is probably right in saying that " In the present passage ' a scatterer ' may be as possible as

(1) *Psalms I,* p. 21.
(2) W. F. Albright, *Yahweh,* p. 6, n. 16.
(3) *Proverbs,* p. 154.

'a crusher', for both 'to scatter' and 'to crush' are common expressions for smiting the enemy". (4)

'al pānayik : "against you". For an understanding of *'al pānayik*, consider E. A. Speiser's rendering of Gen. 25 : 18, *'al p^e^nê kol 'eḥāyw nāpāl*, "and each made forays against his various kinsmen".(5) Presumably the *NEB*'s "against your bastions" is based on a repointing of *'al pānayik* to *'al pinnayik*. Recently also, J. Jeremias (with P. Humbert, *ZAW* 44 [1926] 275 and KB) has adopted the vocalisation *'al pinnayik* — "wider deine 'Zinne'". (6)

nāṣôr m^e^ṣūrāh : "guard your fortifications". As grammarians have long noticed, *nāṣôr* is an infinitive absolute and the equivalent of an imperative. (7) Indeed the succeeding *ṣappēh*, *ḥazzēq* and *'ammēṣ* are also infinitive absolutes — the one addressed, *nîn^e^wēh*, is feminine. (8) *m^e^ṣūrāh*, "your fortifications" does not have a suffix but is probably served by the suffix of *pānayik*. M. Delcor, following Junker, Horst and Haldar, repoints *mṣrh* to *maṣṣārāh*, "la citadelle, la garde" on the basis of Akk. *maṣṣartu*, but he admits that *maṣṣārāh* is "non documenté dans l'A. T.". (9) The LXX *ek thlípseōs* seems to be based on *miṣṣārāh* (*min* + *ṣārāh*). The *NEB*'s "the siege is closing in", is quite unnecessary.

ṣappēh derek : "watch the road". Compare this with Is. 21 : 6, *lēk ha'^a^mēd ham^e^ṣappeh*, "go set a watchman", and Jer. 48 : 19, *'el derek 'im^e^dî w^e^ṣappî*, "stand by the way and watch". In the Babylonian Chronicle, describing events leading up to the fall of Nineveh, the word *ṣāpītu* occurs. According to A. L. Oppenheim, the *ṣāpītu* was "a (wooden) tower used for the siege of a walled town". (10) Cf. Akk. *ṣapû*, "to look out, watch". Perhaps worthy of note is Dahood's version of Lam. 4 : 17, *b^e^ṣippiyyātēnû ṣippînû*, "From our watchtowers we intently watched". (11) The root *ṣpy* possibly occurs

(4) *Studies*, p. 41. Note that Dahood, *Psalms I*, p. 265, refers to *nāpaṣ*, "to shatter, disperse", with ZLH 525a, *contra* BDB 658 f, who posit two distinct verbs, *nāpaṣ*, "to shatter", *nāpaṣ*, "to disperse".

(5) *Genesis*, p. 187, for the translation; pp. 118 and 188 for his notes on the "adversative sense" of Heb. *'al p^e^nê*.

(6) *Kultprophetie*, p. 27.

(7) Cf. GK § 113 bb; *GHB* 356.

(8) Most lexica take *ṣappēh*, *ḥazzēq*, and *'ammēṣ*, as masc. sing. imperatives.

(9) "Nahum", in L. Pirot and A. Clamer, *La Sainte Bible*, VIII/I p. 375.

(10) *ANET* 304, n. 8. For *ṣāpītu*, *CAD* [Ṣ] 97.

(11) *Biblica* 51 (1970) 403.

in *UT*, Krt : 149, *bṣp ʿnh*, " in the gaze of her eyes ", which Dahood compares with Ps. 66 : 7, *ʿênāyw baggôyîm ṭispenāh*, " his eyes keep watch on the nations " (12) and Prov. 15 : 3, *ʿênê yahweh ṣōpôt rāʿîm wᵉṭôbîm*, " The eyes of Yahweh gaze upon the wicked and the good ". (13) Recently, however, de Moor has preferred the connection of Ugar. *ṣp* in *UT*, Krt : 149, with Ar. *ṣafw*, " clearness, purity ". (14) Another possible Northwest Semitic occurrence of the root is Neo-Punic *ṣp*', " seer ". (15)

ḥazzēq motnayim 'ammēṣ kōaḥ mᵉ'ōd : " Strengthen your loins, summon all your strength ". In view of Is. 22 : 21, *wᵉhilbaštîw kuttontekā wᵉ'abnētᵉkā 'ᵃḥazzᵉqennû*, " And I will clothe him with your robe and I will gird your sash on him ", and Prov. 31 : 17, *ḥāgᵉrāh bᵉʿôz motnehā wattᵉ'ammēṣ zᵉrōʿôtehā*, " She girds her loins with strength and makes her arms strong ", perhaps one should translate *ḥazzēq* by " gird ". (16) The Vulg. renders *ḥazzēq motnayim* by " conforta lumbos ", and, consistently, Is. 22 : 21 (see text above), " cingulo tuo confortabo eum ". In fact the versions generally seem to have taken *ḥazzēq* in this verse of Nahum, with its usual meaning " strengthen ". Ugaritic is the only other Semitic language to attest the root *'mṣ* so far : *UT*, 1001 : 14, *amṣ yd*, " strong of hand ". (17)

Pope (18) refers to Nah. 2 : 2 in the long note in his commentary on Job where he discusses the loins as the seat of strength. Fitzmyer translates the phrase *whtḥzq ḥzq t mqwm* (in a Letter of the Bar Cochba period found in Wadi Murabbaʿât) thus : " Take courage and fortify [that] place ". (19)

motnayim : " your loins ". As often with parts of the body, the possessive suffix is not necessary. Cf. commentary on Nah. 3 : 19.

(12) *Psalms II*, p. 121.

(13) *UHP* 70. Cf. also *UT*, Glossary No. 2183.

(14) *Ugarit-Forschungen* 2 (1970) 321.

(15) Consult *KAI*, II, p. 149.

(16) So G. R. Driver, *JTS* 41 (1940) 172. See also his article " Hebrew Poetic Diction ", in *Congress Volume : Copenhagen* 1953, pp. 29-30, where he attributes the use of *ḥzq*, " gird ", in Is. 22 : 21 and Nah. 2 : 2 to Aramaic.

(17) Dahood, *UHP* 51, compares *'mṣ yd* with Job 17 : 9, *ûṭᵉhor yādayim yōsîp 'ōmeṣ*, " the cleanhanded grow in strength ". *Idem*, *Psalms II*, p. 260.

(18) *Job*, p. 271. Cf. also, the comments on Nah. 2 : 11, where we refer to Canaanite descriptions of loss of courage, which mention specifically the loosening and breaking up of the loins. Stonehouse, *Zephaniah and Nahum*, p. 137, has, " make strong your loins ", for the text in Nahum.

(19) " The Bar Cochba Period ", *BCCT* 158, Mur. 44 : 7.

kōaḥ me'ōd compares with *UT*, 54 : 13, *'z mid*, " very strong ". In the Ugar. place name *snr mid*, " Great Snr ", Gordon regards *mid* as an adjective. [20] Note also *UT*, 51 : V : 77,94,100, *mid ksp*, " much silver ", and *UT*, Krt : 88, *ul mad*, " mighty army ".

The repetition of the consonant *ṣ* is interesting in the verse: *mpyṣ – nṣwr – mṣrh – ṣph – 'mṣ*. And note the inversion of the consonants e.g. *mpyṣ – ṣph*.

2 : 3

šāb : " is restoring ". The nuance is that of " restoring fortunes " like that pointed out by Dahood in Ps. 14 : 7 [21] ; 85 : 2 [22] and 126 : 1,4 [23]. He compares Aram. Sefîre, *AIS*, III : 24, *hšbw 'lhn šybt by-[t 'by]*, [24] " The gods restored the fortunes of [my father's house] ", with Ps. 126 : 1, *bešûb yahweh 'et šîbat ṣiyyôn*, " When Yahweh restored the fortunes of Zion ".

'et ge'ôn ya'aqōb kige'ôn yiśrā'ēl : " the glory of Jacob like the glory of Israel ". Because of the mention of *ûzemōrêhem*, " and their vines ", further on in the verse, critics have deemed it necessary to emend *ge'ôn*, " glory ", to *gepen*, " vine ". Thus Delcor writes : " 'leur sarment ' montre clairement que le texte est fautif et qu'il faut lire *gepen*, ' la vigne ', au lieu de *ge'ôn* (Sellin, Horst, Junker, Nötscher, George) ". [25].

Many years ago, J. M. P. Smith wrote that the verse " demands the mention of a vine here as the antecedent of its thought ". [26] The emendation of *ge'ôn* to *gepen* is still accepted in the recent *The Jerome Biblical Commentary*. [27] M. Buttenweiser, in his commentary on the Psalms, is convinced that this verse is an " Exilic addition to the pre-Exilic prophecy of Nahum ", [28] and feels that it is modelled after Psalm 80 ". [29] A. George [30] believes that there is an allusion

(20) *UT*, Glossary No. 1406.

(21) *Psalms I*, p. 82.

(22) *Psalms II*, p. 286.

(23) *Psalms III*, pp. 218, 220.

(24) Dahood's translation, *Psalms III*, p. 218.

(25) " Nahum ", p. 374. See also Kraeling, *Commentary on the Prophets*, II p. 236, for the same emendation.

(26) *CECBN* 305.

(27) Cf. R. T. A. Murphy, " Nahum ", in *The Jerome Biblical Commentary*, p. 294.

(28) *The Psalms*, p. 236.

(29) *Ibid.*

(30) *Michée, Sophonie, Nahum*, p. 88, n. " *d* ".

here to the poem of Is. 5 : 1-7 and that the theme reappears in Ezek. 17 and Ps. 80 : 9. But it seems to the present writer that the emendation of *g*^{e}*'ôn* to *gepen* is audacious.

We have already referred to the repetition of the verb *'umlal* in Nah. 1 : 4. The repetition of *g*^{e}*'ôn* in the present verse is only one of many examples of repetition in Hebrew and Ugaritic. Note the repetition in *UT*, 49 : II : 28-29, *klb arḫ l'glh klb ṯat limrh*, " like the heart of the cow toward her calf, like the heart of the ewe toward her lamb " ; and in *UT*, 52 : 8-9, *bdh ḫṭ ṯkl bdh ḫṭ ulmn*, " in his hand is the staff of bereavement, in his hand the staff of widowhood ".

kî b^{e}*qāqûm bōq*^{e}*qîm :* " For plunderers plundered them ". From the root of *b*^{e}*qāqûm* and *bōq*^{e}*qîm* are probably derived also *bûqah* and *m*^{e}*bûqāh* of verse 11.

An examination of the lexica and Bible translations shows that there is considerable uncertainty (or disagreement rather?) as to the exact meaning of the root or roots involved. Verbal forms from the root *bqq* are found in several prophetical books, Is. 19 : 3 ; 24 : 1,3 ; Jer. 19 : 7 ; 51 : 2 ; Hos. 10 : 1. BDB 122b, lists I *bqq*, " be luxuriant ", Ar. *baqqa*, " be profuse, abundant ", and places Hos. 10 : 1, *bôqēq* under this root ; II *bqq*, " empty ", Ar. *baqqa*, " make a gurgling noise — (as of a vessel being emptied of water) ", cf. *baqbūq*, " flask ". From this second root it derives all occurrences of *bqq* except Hos. 10 : 1. It also derives *bûqāh* and *m*^{e}*bûqāh* (rendered " emptiness ") from this root. KB 144b, posits only one root, *bqq*, " lay waste ", Ar. *bāqa* " effect evil ". *bûqāh* and *m*^{e}*bûqāh* are given the meaning " emptiness " there also. By positing only one root, KB is forced to render Hos. 10 : 1, *gepen bôqēq* by " degenerating vine ". The recent *HALAT* 144, is undoubtedly right in positing two roots. The following represents the present writer's conclusions as they were worked out before the appearance of *HALAT*.

I *bqq*, " be luxuriant ", Ar. *baqqa*, " be loquacious ; be profuse (of heavens giving rain) " ([31]) ; *baqbaqat*^{un} ([32]), " gurgling sound of a mug " (cf. Heb. *baqbūq*, " flask " ; Syr. *bagbūgā*). Hos. 10 : 1, *gepen bôqēq* = " luxuriant vine " ; cf. LXX, *euklēmatousa* ; Vulg. *frondosa*.

([31]) E. W. Lane, *Arabic–English Lexicon* I, p. 233b. H. Wehr, *A Dictionary of Modern Written Arabic*, lists *baqqa*, " give off in abundance " ; *baqqāq*, " loquacious " ; *bqbq*, " gurgle, bubble, chatter, splutter ". Cf. also, P. Humbert, *ZAW* 62 (1949-50) 200.

([32]) Ar. *baqbaqat*^{un} and its cognates are onomatopoeic formations. Cf. H. Fleisch, *Traité de philologie arabe*, I, pp. 403-405. Despite root attachment, one should not decide the meaning of Heb. *bqq* on the basis of Heb. *baqbūq* or Ar. *baqbaqat*^{un}.

II *bqq/bwq* (33) " lay waste; generally cause destruction and harm by attacking things or persons ", etc. " make void ". Ar. *bāqa,* " brought, effected evil, mischief; wronged someone; stole " etc. *baw-ʿūq^{un}* or *dāhiyat^{un} bawʿūq^{un}* " disaster ", or " vehement calamity ". (34) Haldar's convictions regarding *bqq* and its supposed relation to an Akk. word *baqāqu,* " to spread ", (35) are not shared by the present writer. The major Akkadian dictionaries (36) do not support Haldar's claim in any way.

ûz^{e}mōrêhem šiḥētû : " and their vines they destroyed ". *z^{e}mōrê-hem* is usually rendered " their branches " or " their shoots ", and probably means (*pars pro toto*) " vines ". It has already been mentioned in the discussion of *g^e'ôn* ..., that this understanding of *zmryhm* as " their branches, their vines ", has moved scholars to emend *g^e'ôn* to *gepen,* " vine ". Stonehouse unaccountably argues that one would expect *z^{e}mōrōtêhem* as plural of *z^{e}mōrāh,* and therefore emends the text to read *zētêhem,* " their olive yards " ! (37)

The possibility has to be reckoned with that perhaps the verse has nothing to do with " vines " or " branches " or " olive yards ". One might derive *zmryhm* from *zmr,* cognate with Ugar. *ḏmr,* " soldier; some class of troops " (38). Hence *wzmryhm šḥtw* would mean

(33) These could now be added to the list of bilitteral / hollow verbs in GK § 77.

(34) Lane, *Arabic–English Lexicon,* I, p. 276b.

(35) *Studies,* pp. 42, 58.

(36) *CAD* [B] 100, *baqbaqqu,* " small gnat "; *baqīqātu,* pl. only, " a type of groats "; 101, *baqqu,* " gnat "; 323 *buqāqu,* " (little gnat) pers. name ". W. von Soden, *AHw,* 105, *baqīqātu,* " Faules, Morsches ? "; *baqqu,* " (kleine) Mücke "; 139a, *buqāqu,* " kleine Mücke ? ".

(37) *Zephaniah and Nahum,* p. 115.

(38) *UT,* Glossary No. 727. Also *Supplement* to *UT, ad locum.* Heb. *zmr* and Ugar. *ḏmr* have received a fair amount of investigation. Discussions include; F. M. Cross and D. N. Freedman, *JNES* 14 (1955) 243; H. Cazelles, in *Mélanges André Robert,* pp. 135 f.; N. M. Sarna, *HTR* 57 (1964) 347-352.

The existence of such a root is recognized by *HALAT* 263; but the Ugar. counterpart of Heb. *zāmar,* " sing, make music ", is *ḏmr,* not *zmr* as listed by *HALAT* 262. See *UT,* 602: 3-4, *dyšr wyḏmr bknr,* " He sings and makes music on the lyre ". Recently, Dahood, *Psalms II,* p. 74, has pointed out that in Ps. 59 : 18, *'ezzāmērāh,* " am I safeguarded " (MT, *'^{a}zammērāh,* = *NEB,* 'I will raise a psalm'), corresponds to *'eššāmērāh* (" am I protected ") in v. 10 of the same psalm. It is unfortunate that Loewenstamm did not at least discuss Dahood's suggestion in his recent study of Exod. 15 : 2, *ʿzy wzmrt yh, UT,* 602 : 1,9, *arṣ ʿzk ḏmrk,* and Ps. 59 : 18, *ʿzy 'lyk 'zmrh.* Loewenstamm (*VT* 19 [1969] 464-470) believes Exod. 15 : 2, *ʿzy wzmrt* = " my strength and

" and their soldiers they slaughtered ". For *šiḥēt* can be, and is, followed by personal objects, e.g. 2 Sam. 1 : 14 ; Ezek. 5 : 16 ; 20 : 17.

The verb *šiḥēt* is often used in military contexts ; e.g. Jer. 48 : 18, *kî šōdēd mô'āb 'ālāh bāk šiḥēt mibṣārāyik*, " For Moab's destroyer has attacked you, he has destroyed your strongholds ". Cf. Is. 14 : 20 ; Ezek. 26 : 4.

2 : 4

māgēn : " Shields ". Heb. *māgēn* is sing., but of course it must be rendered here by the English plur. The *māgēn* (Ugar.-Phoen. *mgn*) was a small variety of shield probably made of leather and coated with grease (2 Sam. 1 : 2 ; Is. 21 : 5). [39]

gibbōrêhû : " His men ". Viz. the men of the *mēpîṣ*, " the scatterer " of verse 2. For the suffix of *gibbōrêhû*, see also Hab. 3 : 10, *yādêhû*, " its hands " and Job 24 : 23, *'ênêhû*, " his eyes ". Moabite *ymh*, " his days " (*KAI* 181 : 8) would read *yamêh* (so Cross and Freedman) [40] for older **yamayh *yamayhū*.

me'oddām : " are red ". The LXX went astray badly, offering *ex anthrōpōn* for *m'dm*. *'dm* is an old Canaanite verb. Cf. *UT*, Krt : 62,156 ; 1 Aqht : 204, where the verbs all have the notion of " reddening " or " rouging ". *me'oddām* and Nah. 3 : 7, *šoddedāh* are noted by GK p. 143 § 52q, as examples of *o* for *u* in the initial syllable of Pual. Notice that both examples have medial dental *d*.

metullā'îm : " dressed in scarlet ". *metullā'îm* is a pual participle of a denominative verb derived from *tôlā'*, " scarlet stuff " (Akk. *tūltu*). This is the only example of the verb in the Old Testament. The same collocation of the roots *'dm* and *tl'* is found in Is. 1 : 18, *'im ya'dîmû kattôlā'*, " though they are red like scarlet stuff ". An Aramaic letter mentions *gldy twl'*, which probably means " red skins " according to Driver. [41] The obscurity of *UT*, 68 : 4, *tl'm* is hardly sufficient grounds for Haldar's being " suspicious of the translation

my glory ", but probably it should be rendered, " my strength and power ". Cf. J. Blau and J. C. Greenfield, *BASOR* 200 (1970) 12. If Loewenstamm is right in his interpretation, then Nah. 2 : 3 may offer some interesting connections between *ge'ôn*, " glory ", and *zmryhm*.

(39) Cf. R. de Vaux, *Ancient Israel*, pp. 244-245.

(40) *Early Hebrew Orthography*, p. 38, also p. 35 n. 2 ; see also, Z. Harris, *Development of the Canaanite Dialects*, pp. 55 f.

(41) *Aramaic Documents of the Fifth Century B.C.*, pp. 85-86.

commonly accepted " (42) for the Nahum text. The parallelism leaves no doubt as to the meaning of *m^e^tullā'îm*. The LXX, which came to grief with *m'dm*, does not seem to have understood *mtl'm* either and (reading it with *b'š* of the following colon) offers *empaízontas en purí*, " sporting in the fire " (?). Among recent versions and comments, the following are a selection : " The mighty men are gleaming " ! (C. L. Taylor) (43) ; " his troops are incarnadined " (T. H. Gaster) (44), with the comment, " What the prophet means, of course, is that the shields and uniforms of the soldiers were bloodstained. But, by a clever choice of words, he likens these braves to princes stoled in scarlet ". (45) E. G. Kraeling is also a little disturbed by the description of the attacking foe and writes : " The description of the foe is fantastic : red shields, scarlet clothes. In Herod. 7.61 ff. several contingents in the international Persian army wear colorful garments, but scarlet is not mentioned ". (46)

However, consider Ezek. 23 : 5-6 where the Assyrians are described as being " dressed in purple " (*l^e^bûšê t^e^kēlet*) and 23 : 14 where the Babylonians are mentioned thus : " images of the Chaldeans are engraved in vermillion " (*ḥ^a^qūqîm baššāšar*).

b^e^'ēš : " fiery ". Or " flaming-red ". The *b^e^* of *b^e^'ēš* might be explained best as a *beth essentiae.* (47)

p^e^lādôt : " caparisons ". Hapax *p^e^lādôt* has prompted many lengthy discussions. Haldar, having treated the question at length, found that *p^e^lādôt* had " no meaning however ", (48) and leaves it untranslated. It has long been thought to mean " steel " on the basis of Arab.-Persian *fūlād^un^* (cf. also Modern Urdu). (49) But not even the versions are aware of such a meaning. Cf. LXX *ēníai*, " bridles, reins ", and Vulg. *habenae*. Rowley found the suggestion of Tisdall " worth recording " (50) viz. reading *pōl^e^dôt kā'ēš*, " like fire flash the chariots " (51) *pōl^e^dôt* being a fem. pl. (agreeing with collective

(42) *Studies*, p. 44.
(43) " Nahum ", p. 955.
(44) *Myth, Legend, and Custom*, p. 661.
(45) *Ibid.*, p. 727.
(46) *Commentary on the Minor Prophets*, II, p. 236.
(47) Cf. *GHB* 133c.
(48) *Studies*, pp. 44-46.
(49) Almost all lexica and translations take *p^e^lādôt* to mean " steel ". Most recently, KB 761, although defining *p^e^lādôt* as " steel ", advise reading *lappīdôt* (cf. *BH*³). Notice the *NEB*'s poor effort : " like flickering fire ".
(50) *BO* 4 (1947) 60-61.
(51) *Ibid.*

hārekeb), and from a root related to Akk. *parādu*, " be impetuous, hasten " (*r* for *l*). ([52])

The solution proposed here is similar to one offered by M. Dietrich and O. Loretz. ([53]) It is on the basis of Ugar. *pld*, which occurs in *UT*, 1108 : 7 ; 1111 : 12 ; 1112 : 1,7 ; 1113 : 4,7,8. All these texts are lists of various types of cloth or clothing, so *pld* signifies some kind of covering. ([54]) We have shown elsewhere ([55]) that both Ugar. *pld* and *ḫpn* appear in some of these lists of garments and cloth. Now Ugar. *ḫpnt sswm*, found in *UT*, 2049 : 3,7, a list of equipment for horses and chariots, might well give us a hint to the meaning of *pldwt hrkb* in Nahum. As will be shown below, *hārekeb* probably means " the horses ". Hence *pldwt hrkb* would seem to mean something like " the coverings, blankets " or, perhaps, better, " the caparisons of the horses ".

In *UT*, 1111 : 8, *pldm* is found with *mrbdt* (:11), a cognate of Heb. *marbaddîm*, " covers " (Prov. 7 : 16-17). The plurals Ugar. *mrbdt* and Heb. *mrbdm* should stem any objections that Heb. *pldwt* has a different plural form than Ugar. *pldm*. Dahood points out *s^epārôt* in Ps. 71 : 15 ([56]) for more usual *s^epārîm*, and, elsewhere, gives several Ugar. and Phoen. examples : Ugar. *kbkbm/kbkbt* ; *lbnm/lbnt* ; *rašm/rašt* ; *grnm/grnt* ; Phoen. *ymm/ymt*. ([57]) Other Heb. examples are *šānîm/šānôt* ; *hêkālîm/hêkālôt* ; *ʿprm/ʿprt*. ([58])

hārekeb : " the horses ". Usually the word is rendered by " the chariots ". But recently Pope ([59]) has shown that the term *rekeb* can refer to chariots and horses together, or, to the horses alone. He refers to the statement in 2 Sam. 8 : 4 that David hamstrung the *rekeb*, captured from Hadadezer.

b^eyôm h^akînô : " on the day of array ". Parsing *h^akînô* as a hiphil infinitive construct with the 3rd masc. sing. suffix. The verb *kûn* is used in military contexts to express " making preparations, being ready ", and " in position " for beginning battle. Compare

([52]) Cf. *JQR* 4 (1913-14) 102 f.

([53]) *BO* 25 (1968) 100-101, *pld*, " Decke, Überwarf, Teppich? ".

([54]) Consult *UT*, Glossary No. 2045, *pld*, " a kind of garment made of linen or hair " ; *WuS* 2220, " Kleidungsstück ".

([55]) K. J. Cathcart, " Proverbs 30,4 and Ugaritic *ḫpn*, ' garment ' ", *CBQ* 32 (1970) 419, n. 12.

([56]) *Psalms II*, p. 174.

([57]) *UHP* 15. Also *UT*, § 8.9. Add now Ugar. *ḫpnm / ḫpnt*.

([58]) M. Dahood, *Biblica* 50 (1969) 352.

([59]) " A Mare in Pharaoh's Chariotry ", *BASOR* 200 (1970) 56-61. See the comments of M. Dahood, *Biblica* 51 (1970) 397.

Josh. 8 : 4 and Jer. 51 : 12. The most interesting text however is Prov. 21 : 31, *sûs mûkān leyôm milḥāmāh*, " the horse is arrayed for the day of battle ". *mûkān* is the hophal participle of *kûn*.

Taylor's decision to emend *beyôm* to *kayyām* and to render the phrase with the previous colon : " the squadrons of chariots are spread like the sea ", (60) is quite strange.

wehabberōšîm : " And the spears ". On the basis of the ancient versions, many critics read *wehappārāšîm*, " and the steeds ". Haldar (61) suggests a mere repointing of MT *wehabberōšîm* to *wehabbārāšîm* (*b* for *p*). Although the interchange between the labials *b* and *p* in Northwest Semitic is now firmly established, (62) the present writer believes that we do not have a reference to " steeds " in this phrase anyway. The *NEB*, " squadrons of horse ", is quite unacceptable. We prefer to take the MT *wehabberōšîm* literally, " the cypresses ", or " the cedars ". *berōš* could refer to a weapon, probably a spear made of wood. The discussion of the text would not be complete without a reference to Driver's interpretation of *UT*, 51 : VII : 40-41, *ʿn bʿl qdm ydh ktǵḏ arz bymnh*, " Baʿal's eye is towards his hand when the spear swings in his right hand ". (63) To support his rendition of *arz*, literally " cedar ", as " spear ", Driver refers to Nah. 2 : 4 as a parallel.(64) However, there seems to be an entirely different reason for Baʿal's spear being called " cedar ". Most recently, L. R. Fisher and F. B. Knutson (65) have pointed out that in *UT*, 603 : 4 (= RŠ. 24.245) *ʿṣ brq*, " tree of lightning ", we have a reference to Baʿal's spear. They point out that in the art of Ugarit, Baʿal's spear is a bolt of lightning, which, however, looks like a tree at the top. As well as referring to *UT*, 51 : VII : 40-41, they also draw attention to J. Wilson's trans-

(60) " Nahum ", p. 955 ; also p. 962.

(61) *Studies*, p. 46.

(62) Note especially, Dahood, " Comparative Philology Yesterday and Today ", A Review of J. Barr, *Comparative Philology and the Text of the Old Testament*, *Biblica* 50 (1969) 74-75.

Rowley's objection to Haldar's *habbārāšîm*, viz., that a form with *b* would not be used, when a form with *p* is used in Nah. 3 : 3, is not a serious objection, for, as Dahood points out in the above-mentioned review, the forms *ybky* and *wtpky* are found in the same Ugaritic text, *UT*, 608: 10-11 ; 13-14. Rowley's objection is expressed in his review of Haldar's *Studies*, in *BO* 4 (1947) 60.

(63) *CML* 101. Ginsberg, *ANET* 135, has " yew-club " as the equivalent of Driver's " spear ".

(64) *CML* 135.

(65) *JNES* 28 (1969) 157-159, esp. n. 10, which comments on *ʿṣ brq*.

lation of *Papyrus Leyden* 345, recto, iv 12 – v 2 in *ANET* 249 : " Baal smites thee with the cedar tree which is in his hand ". (66)

horʿālû : " are shaking ". This verb is related to the noun *tarʿēlāh*, " reeling, staggering ". E. Dhorme, connecting *horʿālû* with Heb. *reʿālāh*, renders it, " sont voilés ". (67) M. Dahood (68) relates the Heb. personal name *reʿēlāyāh* (Ezra 2 : 2) with the incomplete Ugar. personal name *rʿl*[ ].

Verse 4 consists of a bicolon and a tricolon. The bicolon has a 9/8 syllable count and a 3/3 stress count ; the tricolon has an 8/5/8 syllable count and a 3/2/3 stress count.

2 : 5

baḥûṣôt ... bārehōbôt : " Through the streets ... in the squares ". The same parallelism (but *reḥōbôt // ḥûṣôt*) occurs in Amos 5 : 16, *bekol reḥōbôt mispēd ûbekol ḥûṣôt yōʾmerû hô hô*, " In all the squares there will be wailing, and in all the streets they shall say, ' Alas, alas ' ". These nouns, in both sing. and plur., are common as pairs in parallelism. BDB 932a think that the *reḥōbôt* were " apparently outside the city " and mention Akk. *rêbit Nīna* (cf. Akk. *rêbitu*, " open place "). E. Lipinski, however, writes of Nineveh, " cité qui s'enorgueillissait de ' ses squares ', *rēbātišu*, et dont les vastes dimensions étaient devenues en Israel un sujet de fable (cf. *Jonas*, III, 3 ; IV, 11) ". (69) However, the etymology of *ri/ebītu* is not entirely certain. The *-itu* ending argues a root *ultimae infirmae*, i.e. *rbʿ*, " four ", rather than *rḥb* ; lexical texts make it equivalent of *sila.dagal.la*, " wide street ". (70) If *rebītu*, then, means " street ", BDB's suggestion need not be taken seriously.

yithôlelû : " race wildly ". The hithpolel of *hll* usually means " to act madly, like a mad man ". (71) A good example of the verb used in a context similar to Nahum is Jer. 46 : 9, *ʿalû hassûsîm wehithōlelû*

(66) A different approach is that of Gaster, who, at first, suggested that *wehappārāšim* (for MT, *habberōšîm*) be connected with an Akk. word *puruššu*, " staff ", (*JBL* 63 [1944] 51-52), but has recently rendered the colon thus : " the fir-trees are rustled (as they pass) " ! Cf. his *Myth, Legend, and Custom*, p. 661.

(67) *La Bible de la Pléiade*, II, p. 796.

(68) *Psalms II*, p. 79.

(69) *RB* 73 (1966) 85.

(70) Courtesy of R. Caplice.

(71) Cf. BDB 237 ; ZLH 193 ; *HALAT* 239.

hārekeb, " Attack, horses ! and charge wildly, steeds ! " The translation of J. Bright, " On, you horses ! Roll, you chariots ! " (72) is too tame.

Gordon, *UT*, Glossary No. 769, defines Ugar. *hll* as " shouting ", and tentatively relates it to Heb. *hillēl*, " praise ", but also possibly to Ar. *hilāl*^{un}, " New Moon ". (73) But according to Albright (74), its etymology is obscure. In Is. 14 : 12, *hêlēl* is son of *šaḥar*, (perhaps " Morning Star, son of Dawn ").

hārekeb : " the horses ". As in verse 4, *hārekeb* probably signifies here " the horses ", rather than " the chariots ", though the latter meaning cannot be ruled out. However, Dahood (75) has suggested that *yithôl*^{e}*lû* is more properly predicated of horses than of chariots. He notes *rekeb*//*sûsîm* in Jer. 46 : 9.

The position of *hārekeb* is interesting for it seems to be suspended between :

baḥûṣôt yithôl^{e}*lû*
and *yištaqš*^{e}*qûn bār*^{e}*ḥōbôt*

Thus there is a 7/3/8 syllable count. The next *bicolon* also has a 7/8 syllable count. Notice the two magnificent examples of *chiasmus* in this verse, which are lost on the *NEB*, whose version of verses 4-5 is a disaster and shows scant regard for the text. The neat situation of *hārekeb* completely overrules any attempt to expel it from the text (e.g. *BH*^{3} and the *NEB*).

yištaqš^{e}*qûn :* " they rush to and fro ". This is the solitary instance of the hithpalpel form of *šqq*/*šwq*, and is probably a denominative verb from Heb. *šôq* ; " leg, thigh " = Ugar. *šq*. Cf. also Akk. *sīqu*, " knee " and Ar. *sāq*^{un} " leg " ; *sāqa*, " lead ". The qal of the verb is found in a similar context in Joel 2 : 9, which collocates verbs from *šqq*/*šwq* and *rwṣ*, just as in this verse of Nahum. Dahood (76) has found another occurrence in Ps. 65 : 10. Haldar (77) seeks to establish that *šqq* means " to abound " on the basis of Akk. and Ar., whilst Rowley (78) follows Reider's (79) suggestion that *yištaqš*^{e}*qûn* means, " reverberate " !

(72) *Jeremiah*, p. 302.
(73) Cf. Aistleitner, *WuS* 832, " die Neumondsichel ".
(74) *Yahweh*, p. 187.
(75) *Biblica* 51 (1970) 397.
(76) *Psalms II*, p. 114.
(77) *Studies*, pp. 48-49.
(78) *BO* 4 (1947) 60.
(79) *AJSL* 34 (1917-18) 68.

mar'êhen kallapîdīm : " Their appearance like torches ". One would expect *mar'êhem*, with the masc. rather than the fem. suffix. Perhaps *-hen* was written under the influence of *-ûn* in *yištaqšᵉqûn*. Or was there in fact an alternative masc. form in *-n*, analogous to the possible plurals *û/îna* which may have been used from time to time in Ugaritic? Gordon [80] compares *UT*, 1099 : 4, *ksmn* with late Hebrew *kôsᵉmîn*.

For the simile here, compare Ezek. 1 : 13, *kᵉmar'ēh hallapīdîm*, " like the appearance of torches " ; Dan. 10 : 6, *ûpānāyw kᵉmar'ēh bārāq wᵉʿênāyw kᵉlappîdê 'ēš*, " his face like the appearance of lightning, his eyes like flaming torches ". The force of the simile is clear in the light of verse 4, *bᵉ'ēš pᵉlādôt hārekeb*. Note the consonants of *pldwt* in verse 4 and of *lpydm* in verse 5.

kabbᵉrāqîm yᵉrôṣēṣû : " Like lightning they flash by ". *yᵉrôṣēṣû* is the only example of the polel of *rûṣ*, " to run, charge ". Perhaps one could render it : " charge by ", a nuance of *rûṣ* discussed by Dahood. [81] Ginsberg [82] and Held [83] seem to be right in taking *trẓẓh* in *UT*, 125 : 49 as a derivative of *rwẓ*, " to run ". *UT*, 125 : 46-51, reads : *ǵzr ilḥu [m]rḥh yiḫd byd [ ] rgrh bm ymn [ ]yqrb trẓẓh [ ]k mǵyh wǵlm aḫth šib yṣat*, " The youth Elhau, His lance in his hand takes, His spear in his right hand, and runs out. Even as he arrives, it grows dark : His sister has gone out to draw water " As Held says, the text demands a *verbum movendi*. Gordon tentatively derives *trẓẓh* as an L (= Polel) form of *rwẓ*.[84]

The three verbs in verse 5, *yithôlᵉlû*, *yištaqšᵉqûn*, and *yᵉrôṣēṣû*, are superb examples of what Muilenburg means, when he says that in " such stems as *pᵉʿalʿal*, Pilpel and Hithpalpel, the verb is given a special energy or movement ". [85] More examples will be indicated in the course of this study.

2 : 6

yazkīrū : " are strong ". Consonantal *yzkr* has puzzled scholars continuously. LXX *mnēsthēsontai* and Vulg. *recordabitur* make little sense in the context. The recent version of Gaster, " He recalls (the

(80) *UT*, Glossary No. 1283. F. M. Cross and R. J. Saley, *BASOR* 197 (1970) 48, regard Arslan Tash *qdšn* (Rev. 12) as an Aramaism.

(81) *Psalms II*, p. 68.

(82) *LKK*, 27.

(83) *Eretz-Israel* 9 (1969) 75, n. 36.

(84) *UT*, Glossary No. 2309.

(85) *Congress Volume : Copenhagen 1953*, 101.

past glories of) his braves " ([86]), is questionable, and contrasts sharply with his earlier suggestion that *yzkr* was an " Assyrianism ", ([87]) and that it was related to Akk. *zakāru*, and meant " he musters " ! ([88]) Haldar ([89]) abandons his generally good respect for the consonantal text and suggests *yzbd*, " he bestoweth ", supposedly referring to some ritual meal ! Taylor discovers *ʿēṣîm* in the text and obtains " His nobles are felling timbers ". ([90]) Driver keeps the consonantal text, but unconvincingly tries to show that, on the basis of Ar. and Aram., *yizzakkᵉrû* (*ytzkrw*) should be the reading with the meaning " puff themselves up " ; ([91]) more recently he has suggested *yizzākēr* or *yizzākᵉrû*, " show themselves off ". ([92]) The *NEB* is not sure and offers two versions : " display their prowess ", or : " shout their names".

We have followed the version proposed by Dahood, ([93]) who reads *yazkīrū* and takes it as a denominative verb from *zākār*, " male ", cognate with Ugar. *dakarum*, " man ", which occurs in a quadrilingual vocabulary discovered at Ras Shamra in 1958. ([94]) Dahood finds support for this analysis in Ps. 20 : 8,

> *ʾēlleh bārekeb wᵉʾēlleh bassûsîm*
> *wᵉʾᵃnaḥnû bᵉšēm yahweh ʾᵉlōhênû nazkîr,*
>
> Some through chariots, and others through horses,
> But we through the Name of our God are strong. ([95])

He compares *nazkîr* (emended by many critics to *nagbîr*, cf. *BH*³) from *zākār*, with *nagbîr*, " we are powerful " (Ps. 12 : 5) from *geber*, " man ". Dahood's proposal has been objected to strenuously by M. Himmelfarb ([96]) who claims that *zākār*, " male ", has a biological connotation only, whereas *geber* has a social meaning. He charges that in the whole Bible, no form of *hizkîr* suggests " be strong ". Despite Da-

([86]) *Myth, Legend, and Custom*, p. 662.
([87]) *JBL* 63 (1944) 52.
([88]) *Ibid.*
([89]) *Studies*, pp. 50-51.
([90]) " Nahum ", p. 963.
([91]) *JTS* 39 (1938) 270.
([92]) In *Hebräische Wortforschung*, p. 54.
([93]) *Psalms I*, p. 129 ; *idem*, *Biblica* 45 (1964) 406. Cf. also R. S. Hanson, *The Psalms in Modern Speech*, I, pp. 31, 37.
([94]) Cf. C. F. A. Schaeffer, *AfO* 19 (1959-60) 193-195. The tablet is in Sumerian, Akkadian, Hurrian, and Ugaritic : *NITA : zi-ka-rum : tu-ru-ḫi : da-ka-rum*. See now, *Ugaritica V*, p. 246.
([95]) *Psalms I*, p. 126.
([96]) " Translating the Psalms ", *Commentary* 45 (February 1968) 74.

hood's reply, (97) Himmelfarb (98) voices his preference for the emendations in *BH*³ : *yᵉkarkᵉrû 'addîrāyw,* " his nobles/officers prance/whirl ", or, *yidhᵃrû 'abbîrāyw,* " his war horses gallop " (translations are Himmelfarb's).

'addîrāyw : " His officers ". Heb. *'addîr,* = Ugar. *adr,* "mighty". The root is found in Phoen.-Punic. Note especially, Punic *KAI,* 101 : 4, *'dr ḥmšm,* " Mächtiger der Fünfzig ". (99) A. Guillaume's contention that the Heb. roots *'dr* and *'zr,* " gird ", are " not really distinct, but in the language of Arabic philologists, are *abdāl* or legitimate and recognized equivalents ", (100) is not convincing in the light of Ugar. *adr,* " mighty ", and *mizrtm,* " garment ". (101)

yikkāšᵉlû : " they stumble forward ". Driver writes : " I can only obtain sense by altering *yikkāšᵉlû* to *yiššālᵉkû,* when it will mean " ' launched themselves on their way(s) ' ". (102) Cf. now, the *NEB,* " rushing in headlong career ". There is no doubt that the word is baffling, for *kāšal* in most military contexts has a sense, which would not seem to fit the context in Nahum. Thus in Is. 5 : 27, *'ên 'āyēp wᵉ'ên kôšēl bô,* " none is weary, none stumbles " ; Jer. 46 : 6, *kāšᵉlû wᵉnāpālû,* " they have stumbled and fallen ", *kšl* clearly suggests weariness and lack of progress. In Nahum, perhaps, the implication is that as the men head towards the ramparts, they stumble in their haste. The proximity of *yikkāšᵉlû* with *yᵉmahᵃrû,* " they speed, hasten ", implies advance and progress.

bahᵃlîkôtām : " in their march ". The Ketib *bahᵃlîkôtām* seems to be the basis of *en tais poreía* [*i*]*s* in the Greek text of the Minor Prophets from Naḥal Ḥever, whereas LXX *en tē poreía autōn* is based on the Qere *bahᵃlîkātām.* (103) The military context settles the nuance of *hlk* in this and texts like Judg. 1 : 10 ; 9 : 1 ; Hab. 1 : 6 ; Ps. 68 : 25 ; 138 : 7, as Dahood has stressed, comparing *UT,* Krt : 92, *hlk lalpm,* " They marched by thousands " (104) (in a description of military movements), and Mesha, *KAI* 181 : 14-15, *w'hlk bllh w'ltḥm bh,* " And I marched by night and fought against it ". (105)

(97) " The Psalms in Translation ", *Commentary* 46 (September 1968) 24.
(98) *Commentary* 46 (September 1968) 34-35.
(99) *KAI,* III, Glossar, p. 1.
(100) *Hebrew and Arabic Lexicography,* II pp. 5-6.
(101) Cf. *WuS* 130a ; *UT,* Glossary No. 124.
(102) *JTS* 39 (1938) 270.
(103) Cf. D. Barthélemy, *Les Devanciers d'Aquila,* p. 184.
(104) *Psalms III,* p. 280.
(105) *Ibid.*

ḥômātāh : " towards the wall ". The final *-h* is the *he directionis.* [106] Heb. *ḥômāh* = Ugar. *ḥmt*, pl. *ḥmyt* ; Phoen. *ḥmt*, pl. *ḥmyt* ; Moabite, *ḥmt* ; El Amarna, *ḫumitu.*

wᵉhākēn : and they set up ". As the three preceding verbs are active, one expects an active sense for *w-hkn* too. Therefore instead of reading MT *wᵉhūkan*, hophal, read *wᵉhākēn*, i.e., *w* + hiphil infinitive absolute. [107] The infinitive absolute, continuing a preceding phrase with a finite verb, is well established in Northwest Semitic. [108]

hassōkēk : " the protector ". The *sōkēk* must be some kind of siege-weapon or defence. The verb *sākak*, " to cover, protect ", is found in a military context in Ps. 140 : 8,

yahweh ʾᵃdōnāy ʿōz yᵉšûʿātî
sakkōtāh lᵉrōʾšî bᵉyôm nāšeq,

Yahweh, my Lord, my fortress of safety,
Shelter my head in the day of arms ! [109]

Note the frequency of *k* in this verse : *yzkr/ykšlw/bhlkwtm/whkn/hskk.* We have mentioned already in various places the repetition of consonants or of the same clusters of consonants. There are times when it may be merely conincidental. But one cannot help noticing it for example in a text like *UT*, 51 : IV : 41-43, *tḥmk il ḥkm ḥkmt ʿm ʿlm ḥyt ḥẓt tḥmk.*

2 : 7

šaʿᵃrê hannᵉhārôt niptāḥû : " The sluice-gates of the canals are opened ". Or, " The sluice-gates of the canals have been opened ". Commentators have never given a satisfactory explanation of the phrase *šaʿᵃrê hannᵉhārôt.* We do know that Sennacherib built an aqueduct at Jerwan, north-east of Nineveh. [110] He wanted to increase the water-supplies for the lands and orchards of Nineveh, and archae-

[106] Note especially *UT*, § 11.1 ; Dahood, *UHP* 33, for a discussion of *he directionis.*

[107] I am grateful to Prof. Aelred Cody for this convincing analysis.

[108] Important are : W. L. Moran, " The Use of the Canaanite Infinitive Absolute as a Finite Verb in the Amarna Letters from Byblos ", *JCS* 4 (1950) 169-172 ; J. Huesman, " Finite Uses of the Infinitive Absolute ", *Biblica* 37 (1956) 410-434.

[109] Translation of Dahood, *Psalms III*, p. 300.

[110] T. Jacobsen and S. Lloyd, *Sennacherib's Aqueduct at Jerwan*, especially Chapter 5, " The Water Supplies of Nineveh ", pp. 31-43. I am grateful to Prof. J. van Dijk, for this reference.

ologists have been able to examine the remains of the Bavian-Khosr canal, which Sennacherib cut and built. There are inscriptions on the aqueduct. The Bavian inscription, written about 690, mentions the *bab nāri*, " sluice-gate ". [111] According to T. Jacobsen, a canal could be a natural river ; hence Sennacherib used the term *nāru*, " canalized river ". [112] Is it not possible that Nineveh's attackers opened up sluice-gates, and that a flood occurred, which breached the walls of Nineveh? According to the Babylonian Chronicles, [113] Nineveh fell in August, 612 B.C. There was a classical tradition [114] according to which Nineveh was destroyed by a flood through an exceptional rising of the river Tigris, and D. J. Wiseman [115] wonders if the breach of Nineveh's walls was not from an unusually high flood on the Tigris. But in the month of August, a " flood " is more likely to be the result of the above suggested opening of sluice-gates. For Gaster, *šaʿ^{a}rê hann^{e}hārôt* is another " Assyrianism ". [116]

w^{e}hahêkal nāmôg : " and the palace is melting ". It is difficult to decide on the right nuance. *nāmôg* can have the connotation of " melting away (in fear) ", as for example, in Is. 14 : 31. It might mean " is in commotion ", suggesting the movement of a crowd hither and thither in commotion. Cf. 1 Sam. 14 : 16. A flood might and probably would have both effects. A third nuance is that the palace " is melting " in the mud and water from the flood. The *NEB* has " topples down ".

2 : 8

haṣṣ^{e}bī : " The Beauty ". Consonantal *hṣb* is a major crux. No satisfactory explanation of the word has been forthcoming so far. According to Driver, " the answer to the riddle stares the interpreter in the face, if only he can combine an adequate knowledge of the Greek and Arabic vocabularies with sufficient imagination to explain a rare or unique Hebrew term " ! [117] Driver obtains a meaning " (captive) train " for a noun *haṣṣōb*, which he relates to Ar. *ṣubb^{un}*, " train "

(111) *Ibid*, p. 38.
(112) *Ibid*, p. 41.
(113) C. J. Gadd, *The Fall of Nineveh*, D. J. Wiseman, *Chronicles of Chaldaean Kings.*
(114) Cf. Diodorus, *Bibliotheca Historica*, Book II, Chapter 26 ; Xenophon, *Anabasis*, Book III, Chapter 4.
(115) *Chronicles*, p. 17.
(116) *JBL* 63 (1944) 52.
(117) *JTS* 15 (1964) 296.

of beasts, and " column " of men. See now the *NEB*, " the train of captives ". But this suggestion does not prove more satisfactory [118] than the one already made by F. Zorell [119] to relate *hṣb* to the Heb. noun *ṣāb*, [120] " wagon, litter ", Akk. *ṣumbu, ṣubbu.* [121] It is interesting that the Greek text of the Minor Prophets from Naḥal Ḥever also took *hṣb* to mean " the wagon, chariot ", *hē lampēnē.* [122]

The LXX *hē hypóstasis* seems to have related *hṣb* to Heb. *nṣb*, " stand ". Delcor [123] although accepting with A. van Hoonacker and others that the LXX *hypostasis* suggests a term derived from *nṣb* or *yṣb*, cautiously points out that *maṣṣēbāh*, for example, signifies a " stele ", rather than a " statue " or " image ". Reider [124] sees *hṣb* as a contracted form of *hāʿaṣēbāh*, " female idol ", an epithet of the Assyrian goddess Ishtar. But the supposed omission of ʿ for the sake of euphony, and the description of the omission of the final *h* as a common biblical phenomenon are too much to accept.

The most recent re-examination of the problem is that by H. W. F. Saggs. [125] He analyses *huṣṣab* as Hophal of a verb *nṣb*, cognate with Akk. *naṣābu*, " to suck out " ; hence : " it is sucked out, it is dissolved ". [126] The following *glth* is taken as a noun related to Akk. *gullatu*, " column base " : the whole phrase is then rendered : " Its column-base(s) is/are dissolved. [127] Saggs' analysis of the text is interesting. If *hṣb* does mean " it is dissolved ", then the present writer would be tempted to attach it to the end of verse 7. Thus *wᵉhahêkal nāmôg wᵉhuṣṣab*, " and the palace is melting and is dissolved ". Verse 7 would then have a 10/9 syllable and a 3/3 stress count.

The present writer has followed the suggestion persistently advocated by R. Tournay, [128] to read (with Knabenbauer and G. A. Smith) *haṣṣᵉbī*. I do have doubts about Tournay's assumption of " graphie défective ". [129] *haṣṣᵉbī*, " The Beauty ", would refer to the statue of

[118] Admittedly, Driver does attempt to get around the problem of what seem to be fem. forms of the verbs (unless they are masc. with *-āh* endings).

[119] ZLH, 678.

[120] Cf. Num. 7 : 3 and Is. 66 : 20.

[121] *CAD* [Ṣ] 244.

[122] Cf. Barthélemy, *Les Devanciers d'Aquila*, p. 199.

[123] *VT* 14 (1964) 136. G. Ryckmans, *Muséon* 71 (1958) 130-131, examines Sabean *nṣb*, and concludes that it means " stela ", rather than " image ". But cf. *DISO* 184, and Dahood, *Psalms I*, p. 241.

[124] *JNES* 8 (1949) 104-107, esp. 106.

[125] *JTS* 20 (1969) 220-222.

[126] *Ibid.* 221.

[127] *Ibid.* 221-222.

[128] *RB* 69 (1962) 304 ; *RB* 72 (1965) 428.

[129] *RB* 69 (1962) 304.

Ishtar at Nineveh. The statues of the gods and goddesses were frequently carried off by the enemy. In the Lamentation over the Destruction of Sumer and Ur, we read, line 153, " Inanna was carriedoff from Erech, was brought to enemy territory " (*ANET Supplement* 614).

gull^{e}tāh : " has been stripped ". Or, " uncovered ". So the LXX *apekalúphthē*. One could read (with *BH*[3]) *gāl^{e}tāh,* " has gone into exile ", or " goes into exile ". (130)

w^{e}'amhōtehā : " and her handmaids ". With Heb. *'amhōtehā*, compare Ugar. plur. *amht.* (131) Saggs, having interpreted *glth* as " column-base(s) ", endeavours to establish that *'mhtyh* is an architectural term, " gate-frames ", (132) related to Is. 6 : 4, *'ammôt.*

m^{e}nah^{a}gôt : " are moaning ". *HALAT* 228 (*sub voce hgh*) still clings to the proposed insertion of *hōgôt* after *m^{e}nah^{a}gôt* (cf. *BH*[3]). This is not necessary. *m^{e}nah^{a}gôt* is not related to *nāhag,* " drive, lead ", but should be derived from *nāhag,* " moan ". In Heb., there are probably several triradicals — *nhg, hgh/y, hgg,* — which are all expansions of a Proto-Semitic biradical *hg.* In Hebrew we have *hāgāh,* " mutter, growl ", and *hāgîg,* " utterance ". Compare Ugar. *hg,* "counting, reckoning ", (133) and *UT,* 1001 : rev. 13, *k'ṣm lttn kabnm lthggn,* " when the trees do not give forth (their voice), when the trees do not utter ". (134)

The description of a person moaning like a dove is found elsewhere and is usually expressed by the verb *hāgāh* ; Is. 38 : 14, *'ehgeh kayyônah,* " I moan like a dove " ; Is. 59 : 11,

> *neh^{e}meh kaddubbîm kullānû*
> *w^{e}kayyônîm hāgōh nehgeh,*
> All of us growl like bears,
> We moan all the time like doves.

The latter text from Isaiah is interesting with its parallelism of *neh^{e}meh* and *nehgeh.* Had J. Halévy been alert to this pair of verbs, he probably would not have written concerning the text of Nahum : " avec le Septante *m^{e}nah^{a}môt,* ' gémissent, se lamentent ', au lieu de *mnhgwt,* ' conduisent ' ". (135) " Moaning like doves ", prevents one

(130) So Driver, *JTS* 15 (1964) 298.
(131) *UT,* § 8.8 ; Dahood, *UHP* 15, notes Phoen. pl. *dlht,* " doors ".
(132) *JTS* 20 (1969) 222.
(133) Cf. Dahood, *Biblica* 33 (1952) 219 ; *idem, Psalms I,* p. 7 ; *idem, Psalms II,* p. 177.
(134) *Idem, Psalms I,* p. 29, n. 2.
(135) *Revue sémitique d'épigraphie et d'histoire* 13 (1905) 112.

from emending Ezek. 7 : 16, *ûpāl^{e}ṭû p^{e}lîṭêhem w^{e}hāyû 'el hehārîm k^{e}yônê haggē'āyôt kullām hōmôt 'îš ba'^{a}wōnô*, " And if any survivors escape, they will be on the mountains, like doves of the valleys, all of them moaning, every one over his iniquity ", a text in which *BH*³ (on the basis of the Syriac) emends *hōmôt* to *yāmûtû*. (136) One might compare *hgh-hgg-nhg* (137) with *hmh-hmm-nhm*.

k^{e}qôl yônîm : " like the sound of doves ". Heb. *qôl*, Ugar. *ql* = " sound ". Note Ps. 104 : 12, *yitt^{e}nû qôl*, " (the birds) sing ".

Heb. *yônāh*, " dove ", now has a counterpart in Ugar. *ynt* found in *UT*, 1 : 1 ; 173 : 23, and 613 : 6. Saggs thinks that *yônîm* is related to *yônāh*, " oppressor ", with the technical sense of " those making a military attack ". (138) Alternatively he believes that *k^{e}qôl yônîm* may represent a term *qôl^{e}yôn*, " rams " ! (139)

This type of simile of the " moaning " or " mourning " of a dove is found in some of the oldest ancient Near Eastern literature. Examples include : " May he moan like a dove in its hole " (" The Curse of Agade " [line 118] *ANET Supplement* 649) ; " I mourn like a dove " (" Lamentation to Ishtar " [line 65] *ANET* 384) ; " I moan like a dove all my days " (*ludlul bēl nēmeqi* [Tablet I, line 107] *Babylonian Wisdom Literature* by W. G. Lambert, p. 36).

m^{e}tōp^{e}pōt : " beating ". *m^{e}tōp^{e}pōt* is a denominative polel participle from *tōp*, " timbrel, tambourine ". The *qal* participle occurs

(136) So, also, *HALAT* 240 *sub voce hāmāh*, no. 5, where the emendation is recommended.

(137) KB 598b, 599b, may well be right in connecting *nāhag*, " to moan ", with *nāhaq*, " bray " (Ugar. *nhqt* ; Ar. *nahaqa*). Von Soden, *AHw* 709, lists West Semitic *nhq* with Akk. *nagāgum* " schreien (Esel) ", and Leslau, *JAOS* 89 (1969) 21, commenting on this entry of *AHw*, notes Eth. *nōhōka*, " sigh, groan ".

For Ugar. *nhq*, " bray ", and Akk. *nagāgu*, " bray ", compare the following texts :

anše. gù. dé	*na-gi-gu*	" brayer "
anše. gù. dé	*šá-gi-gu*	" roarer "
anše. gu.$_4$ ud	*ra-qí-du*	" hopper "

UT, Krt : 120-121,	*ḪAR.ra* = *ḫubullu*, 368-370 ; *JNES* 4
lqr ṯigt ibrh (var. *ṯiqt*, 223)	Till the noise of the neighing of his stallion.
lql nhqt ḥmrh	Till the sound of the braying of his he-ass.
	(Translation : *ANET* 144)

(138) *JTS* 20 (1969) 223.

(139) *Ibid.* 224.

in Ps. 68 : 26, *ʿalāmôt tôpēpôt*, " maidens beating tambours ". (140) *UT*, 605 : 1,5, have the phrase *rm tph*, " the sound of his drum ", and a Phoen. inscription from Abydos, *KAI*, 49:7 reads : *'nky psr bn bʿlytn hmtpp*, " I am PSR, son of BʿLYTN the drummer ".

Saggs (141) cannot accept a denominative verb *tpp*, arguing that it does not represent the noise of a " tambourine ", and also that it does not represent the sound of doves, or the action of maidens beating their breasts. His appeal to a different non-denominative verb *tpp*, " to beat " in Old Aramaic is not only unnecessary, but also problematical, for Fitzmyer (142) has questioned the instances of this verb in the Aramaic inscriptions of Sefîre. Saggs renders *mtppt ʿl lbbhn*, " striking rhythmically upon their midst ". (143) (The midst of the " gateframes ", presumably !)

The distress of the women was to be expected. One is reminded of the description of the reaction of the people of Agade after the invasion by the Gutians :

> The old women ceased not (crying) " Oh, my city ",
> The old men ceased not (crying) " Oh, its men ",
> The *galas* ceased not (crying) " Oh, the Ekur ",
> Its maidens ceased not tearing (their) hair.
>
> (" The Curse of Agade " [lines 201-204]
> *ANET Supplement* 650).

No less noteworthy is *UT*, 1 Aqht : 171-172, *ʿrb bkyt bhklh mšspdt bḥẓrh*, " Weeping women enter his palace, wailing women, his court ".

The repetition of the labials in *mtppt ʿl lbbhn* almost thumps out the sound of the women beating on their breasts.

2 : 9

kibᵉrēkat mayim : " like a pool of water ". Heb. *bᵉrēkāh* (see also the Siloam inscription, *KAI*, 189 : 5), Ugar. *brkt* (*UT*, 604 : 6) ; S. Ar. *brkt* ; Ar. *birkat* ; Egyptian *brkt*. The Ugar. variant form *brky* is found in *UT*, 67 : I : 16. L. Alonso Schökel has aptly described this verse of Nahum as an " estupenda comparación ". (144)

mêmê hî' : " its waters ". Reading *mêmê hî'* for MT *mîmê hî'*, with no change in the consonantal text. The various comments on

(140) Dahood, *Psalms II*, p. 147.
(141) *JTS* 20 (1969) 223.
(142) *AIS*, p. 114, concerning Sefîre III : 13.
(143) *JTS* 20 (1969) 223.
(144) *Estudios de Poética Hebrea*, p. 389.

this phrase have been somewhat extraordinary. Haldar states that the " MT is obviously in disorder ", ([145]) but, in almost the same breath, " the MT is almost preserved as it stands, if we accept the reading *mêmehā* and this gives good sense ". ([146]) GK, § 130 dN, also finds that the text is " evidently corrupt ". This has been the general verdict of hebraists and commentators to date. ([147]) An examination of Ugaritic grammar, however, will show that the independent personal pronouns are found in the *casus obliquus*, both accusative and genitive. Several examples are listed by Gordon. ([148]) Thus *UT*, 1 Aqht : 137-138, 143, *diy hyt*, " the pinions of her ", i.e. " her pinions ", and *UT*, 1 Aqht : 115, *diy hmt*, " the pinions of them ", i.e. " their pinions ". Therefore the *hî'* in *mêmê hî'* is an independent personal pronoun. ([149]) Dhorme in his note on this verse illustrated a point perhaps (unconsciously), when he rendered MT *mîmê hî'*, " des jours d'elle ", ([150]) but having arrived so far, he emended the text to *mêmêhā*.

Saggs proposal to read *mêmehā' hammû hannāsîm* (for MT, *mîmê hî' wᵉhēmmāh nāsîm*), which he renders " its waters have put the fugitives into confusion ", ([151]) ruins a magnificent simile.

'imᵉdû 'ᵃmōdû wᵉ'ên mapneh : " Stop ! Stop ! but no one turns back ". The context and vocabulary of these and the preceding words are similar to those of several passages in Jeremiah's oracles against the foreign nations. Jer. 46 : 5, *nôs nāsû* (MT *ûmānôs nāsû*) *wᵉlō' hipnû*, " they flee pell-mell without looking back " (J. Bright, *Jeremiah*, p. 301) ; Jer. 46 : 21, *kî gam hēmmāh hipnû nāsû yaḥdāyw lō' 'āmādû*, " They too turned tail and fled, not one stood his ground ", (J. Bright, *Jeremiah*, p. 304). Cf. also Jer. 49 : 8,24.

The frequency of *m* in this verse is remarkable — no fewer than nine times *mym* – *mymy* – *hmh* – *nsym* – *'mdw* (twice) – *mpnh*.

([145]) *Studies*, p. 55.

([146]) *Ibid.*

([147]) For some fruitless efforts to reconstruct a Hebrew Text on the basis of various Greek versions, cf. J. Weill, " Nahoum, II, 9-12, et Josèphe (Ant., IX xi § 239-241) ", *REJ* 76 (1923) 96-98 ; P. Humbert, " Nahoum 2,9 ", *REJ* 83 (1927) 74-76.

([148]) *UT*, § 6.4.

([149]) See now Dahood, " The Independent Personal Pronoun in the Oblique Case in Hebrew ", *CBQ* 32 (1970) 86-90, with ref. to Nah. 2 : 9 on p. 90.

([150]) *La Bible de la Pléiade*, II, pp. 796-797, n. 9.

([151]) *JTS* 20 (1969) 224.

2 : 10

bōzzû ... bōzzû : " Plunder ... plunder ". (152) The only biblical examples of the imperative of *bāzaz,* " to plunder ". For some reason, the *NEB* has not taken *bōzzû* as an imperative, and renders the whole colon, " Spoil is taken, spoil of silver and gold ". The repetition of *bōzzû* follows immediately the repetition of *ʿimᵉdû* in the previous verse.

wᵉʾên qēṣeh lattᵉkûnāh : " for there is no end to the treasure ". *ʾên qēṣeh* seems to be a favourite phrase of Nahum. It occurs again in 3 : 3 and 3 : 9, but only twice elsewhere in the Hebrew Bible, both occurrences in Is. 2 : 7, where the phraseology resembles that here in Nahum.

Is. 2 : 7, *wattimmālēʾ ʾarṣô kesep wᵉzāhāb*
wᵉʾên qēṣeh lᵉʾōṣᵉrōtāyw
wattimmālēʾ ʾarṣô sûsîm
wᵉʾên qēṣeh lᵉmarkᵉbōtāyw

It's land is filled with silver and gold
and there is no end to its treasures ;
its land is filled with horses
and there is no end to its chariots.

Heb. *ʾên* = Ugar. *in,* as in *UT,* 51 : IV : 50, *in bt lbʿl,* " There is no house for Baal " ; *UT,* 1 Aqht : 117, *in šmt in ʿẓm,* " there is no fat, there is no bone ".

Infrequent *tᵉkûnāh* has an Aram. counterpart in the papyri from Elephantine. (153)

kᵉlî ḥemdāh : " precious things ". Compare Dan. 11 : 8, *ʿim kᵉlê ḥemdātām kesep wᵉzāhāb,* " with their precious vessels of silver and gold ". Cf. also Hos. 13 : 15 ; 2 Chron. 32 : 27. The root *ḥmd* contains the notion of desire and covetousness, (154) especially for precious things, e.g. Deut. 7 : 25 ; Josh. 7 : 21 ; Ps. 19 : 11 ; but sometimes means " precious ", as in Prov. 21 : 20, *ʾôṣār neḥmād,* " precious treasure ". In EA 138 : 126 Akk. *ḫamūdu* glosses Canaanite *yapu.* (155)

(152) On the plundering of Nineveh, see A. Parrot, *Nineveh and the Old Testament,* with reference there to the Babylonian Chronicle.

(153) Cf. *DISO* 328.

(154) The nuance of *ḥmd* implying " covetousness " is illustrated in Phoen. Karatepe, *KAI,* 26 : AIII : 17, *ḥmdt,* " greediness ". Rosenthal, *ANET* 500, renders *ḥmdt,* " good intentions ", but this is strange and off the mark.

(155) *CAD* [Ḫ] 73.

The collocation of *ḥmd* with " silver " and " gold ", both here in Nahum and in Dan. 11 : 8 (quoted above), is strikingly paralleled in *UT*, 51 : V : 77-78, *tblk ǵrm mid ksp gbʿm mḥmd ḫrṣ*, " The mountains shall bring you much silver, the hills choicest of gold ".

This verse is a tricolon with an 8/8/8 syllable count, and 4/3 (4?)/4 stress count. The consonantal pattern is interesting in the first and third cola :

bz/sp/bz/z–b
kbd/kl/kl/ḥmd

2 : 11

bûqāh ûmebûqáh ûmebullāqāh : " Plunder, slaughter, devastation ". The alliteration and assonance are lost in translation, though Alonso Schökel comes close with " saqueo, saquería, saqueamiento ". (156) In a study of assonant expressions, P. P. Saydon (157) illustrates the combination of words derived from the same stem by pointing to *bûqāh mebûqāh* in Nahum and also to Is. 3 : 1, *mašʿēn ûmašʿēnāh* ; Is. 25 : 1, *'emûnāh 'ōmen* ; Deut. 7 : 14, *ʿāqār waʿaqārāh.* No less noteworthy is Is. 22 : 5, *kî yôm mehûmāh ûmebûsāh ûmebûkāh,* " For a day of panic, trampling and dismay ...", also describing the confusion of war, and very expressive, as Saydon (158) observes, with employment of three assonant words.

It is interesting that the only other occurrence of the root *blq* (apart from the personal name *Bālāq,* (159) king of Moab), is found in Is. 24 : 1, in collocation with *bqq*, just as in Nahum. (160) Two verses later (Is. 24 : 3), the proximity of *bqq/bwq* and *bzz* matches that in Nahum. Is. 24 : 3, *hibbôq tibbôq hā'āreṣ wehibbôz tibbôz,* " The earth shall be utterly plundered and utterly dispoiled ". Isaiah's use of alliteration and assonance compares with that of Nahum.

P. Humbert expels *mebûqāh* from the text, considering it to be superfluous " au point de vue du rythme ". (161) But, the 11/9/9/10 syllable count, and the 4/4/4/4 stress count of this verse, show that his decision is an unfortunate one.

welēb nāmēs ûpîq birkayim ... ûpenê kullām qibbeṣû pā'rûr, " and melting hearts and trembling of knees ... and the faces of all gather

(156) *Estudios de Poëtica Hebrea*, p. 437.
(157) *Biblica* 36 (1955) 38-39.
(158) *Ibid.*, 303.
(159) Num. 22 : 2-24 : 25 ; Josh. 24 : 9 ; Judg. 11 : 25 ; Mic. 6 : 5.
(160) Cf. also, O. S. Rankin, *JTS* 31 (1930) 285.
(161) *AfO* 5 (1928-29) 18.

paleness". The greater part of this verse is a typical Northwest Semitic description of people losing courage and being sick with fear. It should be compared with Is. 13 : 7-8,

ʿal kēn kol yādayim tirpenāh
w^{e}kol l^{e}bab '^{e}nôš yimmās
w^{e}nibbālû ṣîrîm waḥ^{a}bālîm y^{e}'ūḥ^{a}zûn [162]
kayyôlēdāh y^{e}ḥîlûn
'îš 'el rēʿēhû yitmāhû
p^{e}nê l^{e}hābîm p^{e}nêhem

Therefore all hands will be feeble
and every man's heart will melt,
and they will be dismayed; they will be
seized by pangs and agony;
they will be in anguish (or " will writhe ")
like a woman in travail.
They will look aghast at one another;
their faces will be aflame.

Both texts mention the melting of hearts (cf. Josh. 2 : 11 ; 5 : 1 ; 7 : 5 ; Is. 19 : 1 ; Ezek. 21 : 12 [*lēb nāmēs*] ; Ps. 22 : 15). The *NEB* has " courage melting ", a weak translation of *lēb nāmēs* in this particular passage. In Nahum, there is mention of the trembling of the knees ; in the Isaiah text, the feebleness of the hands. Anguish in the loins and the change of the colour of the face are found in both passages. For anguish in the loins, compare also Is. 21 : 3. *ḥalḥālāh* (only 4 times in the O. T.), is derived from *ḥyl/ḥwl*, " to give birth, have labour pains ". The root occurs in *UT*, 75 : I: 25, *ḥl ld*, " go into labour, bear! ", a pair which is found for example in Is. 66 : 8. [163] In Akk., the verb *ḫâlu* means " to be in labour ", [164] and *ḫallu* signifies " the crotch, region between the thighs ". [165] Held [166] calls attention to Akk. *ḫâlu/(w)alādu*.

[162] Reading *qal* passive (for MT, *yō'ḥēzûn*). Cf. Dahood, *BCCT* 63, who reads, in Job 18 : 20, *w^{e}qadmōnîm 'ūḥazû* (MT *'āḥ^{a}zû*) *śāʿar*, " And they of the east are seized by horror ", and suggests *qal* passive in Is. 13 : 8, also.

[163] Other examples are found in Deut. 32 : 18 ; Is. 23 : 4 ; 26 : 17-18 ; 45 : 10 ; 54 : 1 ; Ps. 90 : 2 ; Job 15 : 7 ; 39 : 1. Cf. Dahood, *Psalms II*, p. 323 ; and the detailed notes of Held, *Eretz-Israel* 9 (1969) 78, n. 60, 61.

[164] *CAD* [Ḫ] 55. *ḫâlu* C, " to be in labor ", is probably connected with *ḫâlu* B, " to tremble, writhe ". Note, in fact, that the *NEB* prefers to render Heb. *w^{e}ḥalḥālāh b^{e}kol motnayim*, " writhing limbs ".

[165] *CAD* [Ḫ] 45 .

The exact significance of *qibbeṣû pā'rûr* is not clear. The phrase is found once elsewhere in Joel 2 : 6 where it balances *yaḥîlû*, " they are in anguish ", or " they tremble ". *pā'rûr* is often given the meaning " paleness ". Compare also *BJ*, " perdent leur couleur ", which is an inaccurate version anyway. Contrast GB 632, which gives "Röte" (" redness ") ; KB 750b, " glow ", with the explanation that the ' of *pā'rûr* helps distinguish that word from *pārûr*, " cooking-pot ". But " paleness " is probably the meaning of *pā'rûr* in Nahum. Consider the description in Jer. 30 : 6, *maddûaʿ rā'îtî kol geber yādāyw ʿal ḥalāṣāyw kayyôlēdāh wenehepekû kol pānîm leyērāqôn*, " Why then do I see every man with his hands on his loins like a woman in labour? Why has every face turned pale? " (*RSV*) (167) and the following version of an Akk. text, which *CAD* [Ḫ] 189 quotes under *ḫīlū*, " labour pains : " has my face become *dark* on the day of my labour? ". The distinction between *pā'rûr*, " glow ", and *pārûr*, " cooking-pot ", posited by KB 750b is questionable in the light of the LXX *hōs próskauma chútras* (Joel 2 : 6 also), and Vulg. *sicut nigredo ollae*.

D. R. Hillers (168) has made a study of the Hebrew descriptions of reaction to unfavourable news. An extrabiblical parallel to the description in this verse occurs in *UT*, ʿnt : III : 29-32, *bh pʿnm tṭṭ bʿdn ksl tṯbr ʿln pnh tdʿ tǵṣ pnt kslh anš dt ẓrh*, " Her (Anat's) feet stumble, behind her loins do break ; above her face sweats ; the joints of her loins shake ; weakened are those of her back ". (169)

2 : 12

ûmeʿārāh : " and the cave ". All representatives of the text, including the scroll from Wadi Murrabaʿât, read *mrʿh*, " pasturage ", " meadow ". The text should surely read *meʿārāh*, " cave ", which is a perfect parallel to *meʿôn*, " den ", of the first colon. " Cave " also makes more sense.

One has to exhaust all possibilities for MT *mirʿeh*. A. B. Ehrlich writes : " Auch hier ändert Wellhausen fälschlich *mirʿeh* in *meʿārāh* denn abgesehen davon, dass letzteres Nomen niemals als Bezeichnung für das Lager eines wilden Tieres vorkommt, passt *hw'* wegen seines

(166) *Eretz-Israel* 9 (1969) 78, n. 61.

(167) *Ibid.* 78.

(168) *ZAW* 77 (1965) 86-89. As well as the texts discussed above, Hillers lists Jer. 6 : 22-23 ; 49 : 23 ; 50 : 43.

(169) Cf. Ginsberg, *LKK* 46 ; Dahood, *PNWSP* 29 f. ; *idem*, *Psalms I*, p. 281, on this question.

Genus nicht dazu ". [170] The lion did go to the pasture to seek his prey, and the *kᵉpīrîm* [171] could also hunt for themselves as is suggested say, in Ezek. 19 : 6, *kᵉpîr hāyāh wayyilmad liṭrop ṭerep*, " he became a young lion and learned to catch prey ". Furthermore, *mirʿeh* could refer to any open country where animals, both wild and domestic could feed. In the Proto-Sinaitic inscriptions, there is a text which tells us that the miners of *Serābîṭ el-Khâdem* worshipped *ḏldy mrʿt*, " O (thou) in whose care is the meadow (or pasturage) ",[172] probably Osiris, according to W. F. Albright. [173] From the other texts we know that the miners offered " the wild cow " (*'rḫt*) and " the wild ewe " (*ṯ't*) to the divinities they worshipped. [174] In one text, a prayer reads : *mṯṯʿ lṯt lb*['*t*(*m*)], " Thou who didst save (me) from two lio[nesses] ". [175] However, in Nahum, the end of the verse reads : *wᵉ'ên maḥᵃrîd*, " and none to frighten them away ". Nahum seems to have *mᵉʿārāh* rather than *mirʿeh* in mind.

lābî' : " lioness ". *'aryēh* is " lion ", and *gûr 'aryēh*, " the lion's cubs " in the next colon, so that *lābî'* would be " lioness ", to complete the family !

The versions (LXX *tou eiseltheín*, Vulg. *ut ingrederetur*) seem to have read *lābô'* rather than *lābî'*. The Biblical quotation in 4QpNah has *lby'*, but the pesher seems to interpret the text as the versions have done. [176] Haldar [177] follows Ehrlich, and takes *lby'* as a short form of *lhby'*. The reading *lby'* is found in the scroll of the Minor Prophets from Wadi Murrabaʿât.

wᵉ'ên maḥᵃrîd : " and none to frighten them away ". *'ên maḥᵃrîd* is often found in the descriptions of animals and birds being left undisturbed. Cf. Lev. 26 : 6 ; Deut. 28 : 26 ; Is. 17 : 2 ; Jer. 7 : 33 ; Ezek. 34 : 28 ; Zeph. 3 : 13. Alonso Schökel calls this final phrase the

(170) *Randglossen*, p. 295.

(171) Speiser, *Genesis* p. 365, writes : " The several biblical synonyms for ' lion ' designate various breeds (e.g., the Asiatic as opposed to the African) ". But E. Ullendorff, *VT* 6 (1956) 192, has already opposed similar notions.

(172) *PSID*, Text 346, p. 17.

(173) *PSID*, p. 14.

(174) *PSID*, Texts (349), (352), 353, 365b.

(175) *PSID*, Text 352.

(176) So J. Carmignac, *Les Textes de Qumran*, II, p. 85 ; J. M. Allegro, *Discoveries in the Judaean Desert of Jordan, V*, pp. 38-39 ; pl. XII. Contrast A. Dupont-Sommer, *Semitica* 13 (1963) 64 ; J. Strugnell, *Revue de Qumran*, No. 26 (1970) 207.

(177) *Studies*, p. 61.

" ascendencia clásica ". [178] The root *ḥrd* appears in Neo-Punic, *KAI*, 145 : 5, *bʿl ḥrdt*, " Lord of Terror ".

2 : 13

bedê : " for the needs of ". A. Dupont-Sommer [179] (with Gaster) believes that, in the commentary in 4QpNah, *bdy* = *baddê* (cf. Job 18 : 3), " limbs of ... ", rather than *bedê*, " for the needs of ... "

gōrôtāyw : " his cubs ". This form is not found elsewhere. Jer. 51 : 38, *kegôrê* (some MSS *kegûrê*) *'arayôt*, " like lions' cubs " // *kakkepîrîm* " like young lions ", suggests that the absolute is *gōr*. Therefore, here in Nahum, one might expect *gōrāyw* rather than *gōrôtāyw*. In fact, 4QpNah has *gwryw*. But in Heb., as in Ugar., a masculine noun or feminine noun without a feminine form in the singular, can take the feminine form in the plural. [180] If *gōrāyw* were the right reading, then the verse would have four cola, each with 8 syllables. By keeping MT *gōrôtāyw*, one has an extra syllable in the first colon. Note that in the previous verse, *gûr* occurs.

ûmeḥannēq : " and strangled ". Smith offers " rend " ; [181] Haldar, " rent " ; [182] and *The Jerusalem Bible*, " tore up ". Haldar, [183] to support his translation, invokes Akk. *ḫanāqu*, but this word too, means " to strangle, constrict, compress ". [184] Heb. *ḥnq* is used in 2 Sam. 17 : 23 of Ahithopel hanging himself, and the noun *maḥanāq*, " strangling ", is found in Job 7 : 15. [185] In Phoen. Arslan Tash, *KAI*, 27 : 4-5, there is the phrase *lḥnqt 'mr*, " O strangler of lambs ", [186] and in Ugaritic, one finds *iltm ḫnqtm*, " the two strangling goddesses " (cf. *UT*, 1 : 18 and 614 : A : 13). The LXX *apépnixe* also shows that " strangled " is the likely meaning. Lions do strangle their prey and we have excellent representations from the Near East of lions strangling their prey. Most impressive is a Phoenician ivory (c. 715 B.C.)

(178) *Estudios de Poética Hebrea*, pp. 424-425.

(179) *Semitica* 13 (1963) 64-65. Cf. also, J. Strugnell, *Revue de Qumran* No. 26 (1970) 208. But see now, Y. Yadin, *IEJ* 21 (1971) 12.

(180) *UT*, § 8.8.

(181) *CECBN* 325.

(182) *Studies*, p. 83.

(183) *Studies*, p. 61.

(184) *CAD* [Ḫ] 77. Note also, *ḫāniqu*, " strangler ", *ibid.*, 80.

(185) Consult Pope, *Job*, p. 57.

(186) Cf. Dahood, *Orientalia* 34 (1965) 87 ; more recently, F. M. Cross and R. J. Saley, *BASOR* 197 (1970) 44, 47.

in the British Museum, [187] which shows a lioness standing over a man with its left paw around his neck. Even older, on a shell, dating from the 3rd millennium B.C., and excavated at Lagash, there is a scene of a lion attacking a bull. [188] The lion has its paw and foreleg right around the bull's neck, and its teeth buried in the back of its neck.

ḥōrāyw : " his caves ". *ḥōr*, " cave " or " hole ". Cf. 1 Sam. 14 : 11, and Job 30 : 6. Recently, *HALAT* 335a, has compared Is. 11 : 8, *'al ḥūr pāten*, " over the hole of the serpent ", with Ugar. *ḫr b ṯnm*. But there are two difficulties here. First, *ḫr b ṯnm* is an emendation of *ḫw b ṯnm*, proposed by Virolleaud. Secondly, *HALAT* 334b has already related Heb. *ḥōr* to Ugar. *ḫr*, *ḫrt*, " hole, grave ".[189] Gordon informs us that Virolleaud renders RŠ 24.247, *ḫr apm*, " nostrils ". [190] H. A. Hoffner would relate Heb. *ḥōr*, *ḥūr*, to Hittite **hura*, " perforation (?), hole ". [191]

ṭᵉrēpāh : " torn flesh ". As we have rendered *ṭerep*, " prey " in the previous colon, it seems better to keep a different word for *ṭᵉrē-pāh*. The root *ṭrp* appears no fewer than 3 times in this verse, and occurs once again in the next verse. Noteworthy is the *chiasmus* and the a b c // c′ b′ pattern in

wayᵉmallē' ṭerep ḥōrāyw
ûmeʿōnōtāyw ṭᵉrēpāh

Dahood has noted the same pattern : single verb + chiastic arrangement, in Ps. 126 : 2,

'āz yimmālē' śᵉḥôq pînû
ûlᵉšônēnû rinnāh
Then our mouth was filled with laughter,
and our tongue with shouts of joy. [192]

and *UT*, 51 : IV : 10-11,

št gpnm dt ksp
dt yrq nqbnm

[187] See A. Parrot, *The Arts of Assyria* (New York 1961), figs. 186 and 187.
[188] S. N. Kramer, *History Begins at Sumer*, Pl. 9, opposite p. 132.
[189] E. Ullendorff, *JSS* 7 (1962) 342, equates Ugar. *ḫrt* with Heb. plur. *ḥōrîm*, taking *ḫrt* as a masc. with fem. plur. termination.
[190] *UT*, Glossary No. 998.
[191] *Orientalia* 35 (1966) 389.
[192] *Psalms III*, p. 219.

He put a harness of silver,
of gold, trappings : [193]

2 : 14

hinᵉnî 'ēlayik : " Behold I am against you ". The particle *hinᵉnî* brings the poem to a climax and marks the culmination of the unit, verses 2-14. [194]

rikbāh : " your chariots ". The LXX *plēthos sou* suggests *rubbēk*, " your multitude ", or " your abundance, wealth ", and indeed 4QpNah has *rwbkh* in the *pesher* of this verse. Perhaps consonantal *rkbh* should be parsed as *rekeb* + the accusative ending. It could be served then by the doubleduty suffix of *kᵉpîrayik*. A similar situation is found in several biblical passages. [195]

tō'kal ḥāreb : " and the sword will devour ". Compare Deut. 32 : 42, *wᵉḥarbî tō'kal bāśār*, " and my sword will devour flesh ". [196]

ûkᵉpîrayik : " and your young lions ". In other words, " your warriors ". Several scholars have pointed out how animal-names in Hebrew are used metaphorically to denote dignitaries and various classes of people. [197] For example, *'abbîr*, " bull ", but also " king ", or " prince " ; *kᵉpîr*, " young lion ", or " warrior ". And in Ugar. *ṯr*(*m*), " bulls ", but also " peers " ; and *ẓby*(*m*), gazelles ", but also " barons ". [198] Ps. 34 : 11, *kᵉpîrîm rāšû wᵉrāʿēbû wᵉdōrᵉšê yahweh lō' yaḥsᵉrû kol ṭôb*, is rendered by Dahood : " The rich will grow poor and hungry, but they who seek Yahweh will lack no blessing ". [199] Dahood would regard *kpyrym* as either a by-form of *kabbîrîm*, " magnates ", or the word for " young lions ", used metaphorically. [200] Likewise Dahood would render Ezek. 38 : 13, *wᵉsōḥᵃrê taršîš wᵉkol*

[193] *Ibid.*

[194] On the role of the particle *hinnēh*, consult Alonso Schökel ", *Biblica* 37 (1956) 74-80 ; Muilenburg, *JBL* 88 (1969) 14-15.

[195] On the double-duty suffix with nouns — the suffix omitted in the first colon, see Dahood, *Psalms III*, p. 429.

[196] Cf. van Dijk, *Ezekiel's Prophecy on Tyre*, p. 11, and see our commentary on Nah. 3 : 15.

[197] Especially Dahood, *Biblica* 40 (1959) 160-170 ; P. D. Miller, *Ugarit-Forschungen* 2 (1970) 177-186.

[198] So Ginsberg, *LKK* 42. Cf. also Rosenthal, *Orientalia* 16 (1947) 401-402 on Amos 4 : 1, *pārôt habbāšān*.

[199] *Psalms* I, p. 204.

[200] *Ibid.*, p. 206.

k^epîrehā, " and the merchants of Tarshish and all its magnates ". ([201]) Thus, in the latter text, there is no need to emend *k^epîrehā* to *rōk^e-lehā*, " its traders ", just as there is no necessity to emend *ûk^epîrayik* in Nahum to *ûgibbōrayik* (cf. *BH*³). R. Schiemann ([202]) takes *k^epîrîm* as " princes ", in Ezek. 19 : 2-6 and Nah. 2 : 12-14. Failure to recognise the figurative use of *k^epîr*, led J. M. P. Smith to write about this verse : " MT has ' her chariot ', for ' thy lair ' ; but this does not suit the figure of the lion which continues here, as is clear from the latter part of the line ; while GS [Greek, Syriac] reflect a different text from MT and open the door for emendations " ! ([203]) G. R. Driver has a similar problem and surpasses many previous critics in his ingenuity, arguing that *rkbh* is " impossible ", both in form and meaning because of its parallelism with *kpyryk* ; hence he emends *rkbh* to *rhbk* " thy pride ", ([204]) a suggestion which has found its way into the *NEB*. E. G. Kraeling entertains similar suspicions : " the burning of chariots interferes with the figure of the lions and could be misplaced ". ([205])

Just as *k^epîrayik* pairs off with *rikbāh* in Nahum, so in difficult Panammū II, *KAI*, 215 : 10, one finds *bʿly kpyry/wbʿly rkb*, which *KAI* translates : " Besitzer von *Ortschaften* und Besitzer von Streitwagen ". ([206]) Nothing can be said for the moment because of the difficulties in the inscription, but future research may reveal something interesting.

w^elō' yiššāmaʿ ʿôd qôl mal'ākāyik : " and the voice of your messengers will be heard no more ". Compare Ezek. 26 : 13, *w^eqôl kinnôrayik lō' yiššāmaʿ ʿôd*, " the sound of your lyres will not be heard again ", which in turn resembles Aramaic Sefîre, *AIS*, I : A : 29, *w'l ytšmʿ ql knr b'rpd wbʿmh*, " Nor may the sound of the lyre be heard in Arpad and among its people ". ([207])

MT *mal'ākēkēh* is strange. The final *h* could be due to dittography (cf. 3 : 1, *hôy*). Therefore read *mal'ākāyik*. There is no 2nd pers. fem. suffix in *kh*, even though M. Martin ([208]) thinks he finds

([201]) *Ibid.*

([202]) *VT* 17 (1967) 367-369, though the equation of *k^epîrîm* in Neh. 6 : 2 with " princes " is doubtful. Cf. J. M. Myers, *Ezra, Nehemiah*, p. 135, who leaves it as a proper name.

([203]) *CECBN* 326.

([204]) *JTS* 39 (1938) 271.

([205]) *Commentary on the Prophets*, II, p. 238.

([206]) *KAI*, II, p. 224.

([207]) The translation is that of Hillers, *Treaty-Curses*, p. 57. Fitzmyer, *AIS*, p. 15, reads *wbʿmh*, " but among its people ", as the beginning of the following sentence.

([208]) *Muséon* 70 (1957) 127-144.

it in a Qumran Isaiah scroll. Heb. *mal'āk* = Ugar. *mlak*. Note also Ugar. *mlakt*, " mission, embassy ". (209) Compare also *AIS*, III : 8, *w'šlḥ ml'ky '[l]wh lšlm*, " when I send my ambassador to him for peace ". The LXX *tà érga sou* is based on a connection of consonantal *ml'kkh* with *m^{e}lā'kāh*, " work ". Driver's *ma'^{a}kālēk*, " thy feeding ", (210) is far-fetched, but has now been incorporated into the *NEB*.

(209) E.g., *UT*, 1012 : 33-36, *w mlk b'ly bnš bnny 'mn mlakty hnd ylak 'my*, " And O king, my lord let my agent together with my messengers be sent here to me ". Version of Albright, *BASOR* 150 [1958] 38).

(210) *JTS* 39 (1938) 271.

CHAPTER III

Nahum 3 : 1-19

Text: Nahum 3:1-4

Syllable Count	Stress Count		
4	3	1	הוֹי עִיר דָּמִים
4	2		כֻּלָּהּ כַּחַשׁ
5	2		פֶּרֶק מְלֵאָה
5	3		לֹא יָמִישׁ טָרֶף
8	5	2	קוֹל שׁוֹט וְקוֹל רַעַשׁ אוֹפָן
4	2		וְסוּס דֹּהֵר
8	4		וּמֶרְכָּבָה מְרַקֵּדָה
5	2	3	פָּרָשׁ מַעְלֶה
10	4		וְלַהַב חֶרֶב וּבְרַק חֲנִית
9	4		וְרֹב חָלָל וְכֹבֶד פָּגֶר
8	4		וְאֵין קֵצֶה לַגְּוִיָּה
8	4		יִכָּשְׁלוּ בַּגְּוִיּת
7	3	4	מֵרֹב זְנוּנֵי זוֹנָה
9	4		טוֹבַת חֵן בַּעְלַת כְּשָׁפִים
11	4		הַמְּכֶרֶת גּוֹיִם בִּזְנוּנֶיהָ
9	4		וּמִשְׁפָּחוֹת בִּכְשָׁפֶיהָ

Translation: Nahum 3:1-4

1 Woe to the city of blood,
all full of lies;
full of plunder,
prey is not lacking.

2 The sound of the whip and the sound of the rumbling wheel,
and galloping horse,
and jolting chariot,
3 charging spanhorse.

Flash of the sword and gleam of the spear,
a multitude of slain a mass of corpses;
there is no end to the bodies,
they stumble over the bodies.

4 Because of the numerous harlotries of the harlot,
of fair appearance, a mistress of sorceries;
Who is known by the nations for her harlotries,
and by the clans for her sorceries.

Text: Nahum 3:5-8

Syllable Count	Stress Count		
		5	הִנְנִי אֵלַיִךְ
			נְאֻם יַהְוֶה צְבאוֹת
11	4		וְגִילֵּתִי שׁוּלַיִךְ עַל־פָּנָיִךְ
8	3		וְהַרְאֵיתִי גוֹיִם מַעְרֵךְ
7	3		וּמַמְלָכוֹת קְלוֹנֵךְ
10	4	6	וְהִשְׁלַכְתִּי עָלַיִךְ שִׁקֻּצִים
10	4		וְנִבַּלְתִּיךְ וְשַׂמְתִּיךְ כְּרֹאִי
7	3	7	וְהָיָה כָל־רֹאַיִךְ
7	3		יִדּוֹד מִמֵּךְ וְאָמַר
6	2		שָׁדְדָה נִינְוֵה
4	3		מִי יָנוּד לָהּ
6	3		מֵאַיִן אֲבַקֵּשׁ
5	3		מְנַחֲמִים לָךְ
8	3	8	הֲתֵיטְבִי מִנֹּא אָמוֹן
8	3		הַיֹּשְׁבָה בַּיְאֹרִים
5	3		מַיִם סָבִיב לָהּ
4	3		אֲשֶׁר חֵיל יָם
5	3		מַיִם חוֹמָתָהּ

Translation: Nahum 3:5-8

5 Behold I am against you —
Oracle of Yahweh Sabaot —
And I am going to lift your skirts over your face,
and I will show the nations your nakedness,
and the kingdoms your shame.
6 And I will throw filth at you,
and treat you with contempt and make you a spectacle.

7 And it will happen that every one who sees you,
will go away from you and say:
Nineveh is ruined,
who will grieve for her?
Where will I seek
comforters for you?

8 Are you better than No-Amon,
seated by the Nile,
Water surrounding her;
whose outer-wall was the sea,
water her ramparts?

Text: Nahum 3:9-11

Syllable Count	Stress Count	Verse	Text
3	2		כּוּשׁ עָצְמָה
8	3	9	וּמִצְרַיִם וְאֵין קֵצֶה
4	2		פּוּט וְלוּבִים
6	3		הָיוּ בְּעֶזְרָתֵךְ
5	2	10	גַּם־הִיא לַגֹּלָה
6	2		הָלְכָה בַשֶּׁבִי
9	4		גַּם עֹלָלֶיהָ יְרֻטְּשׁוּ
5	2		בְּרֹאשׁ כָּל־חוּצוֹת
6	2		וְעַל־נִכְבַּדֶּיהָ
4	2		יַדּוּ גוֹרָל
6	2		וְכָל־גְּדוֹלֶיהָ
6	3		רֻתְּקוּ בַזִּקִּים
6	3	11	גַּם־אַתְּ תִּשְׁכְּרִי
6	3		תְּהִי נַעֲלָמָה
6	2		גַּם־אַתְּ תְּבַקְשִׁי
5	2		מָעוֹז מֵאוֹיֵב

Translation: Nahum 3:9-11

9 Cush was her strength
and Egypt too, without limit;
Put and the Libyans
were in your army.

10 Yet she went into exile,
she went into captivity;
Her little ones were dashed to pieces
at the head of every street.

And they cast lots
for her nobles;
And all her great men
were bound in chains.

11 You also will hire yourself out
you will become young again;
You also will seek
refuge from the enemy.

Text : Nahum 3 : 12-15a

Syllable Count	Stress Count		
8	3	12	כָּל־מִבְצָרַיִךְ תְּאֵנִים
4	2		עם בִּכּוּרִים
8	3		אִם־יִנּוֹעוּ וְנָֽפְלוּ
4	2		עַל־פִּי אוֹכֵל
9	4	13	הִנֵּה עַמֵּךְ נָשִׁים בְּקִרְבֵּךְ
7	3		לְאֹיְבַיִךְ פָּתוֹחַ
8	3		נִפְתְּחוּ שַׁעֲרֵי אַרְצֵךְ
8	3		אָֽכְלָה אֵשׁ בְּרִיחָיִךְ
7	3	14	מֵי מָצוֹר שַׁאֲבִי־לָךְ
7	2		חַזְּקִי מִבְצָרָיִךְ
4	2		בֹּאִי בַטִּיט
7	3		וְרִמְסִי בַחֹמֶר
6	2		הַחֲזִיקִי מַלְבֵּן
5	3	15	שָׁם תֹּאכְלֵךְ אֵשׁ
5	2		תַּכְרִיתֵךְ חֶרֶב
6	2		תֹּאכְלֵךְ כַּיָּלֶק

Translation: Nahum 3:12-15a

12 All your fortifications are fig-trees,
your troops early figs;
If they are shaken, they fall
into the mouth of the eater.

13 Behold your troops are women in your midst,
the gates of your city are opened,
opened wide to your enemies;
fire consumes your bars.

14 Water for the siege draw for yourself,
strengthen your fortifications;
Go into the brick-clay,
and tread the mortar;
take hold of the brick-mould.

15 Behold fire will devour you
the sword will cut you off,
it will devour you like the young locust.

Text: Nahum 3:15b-18

Syllable Count	Stress Count		
7	3	הִתְכַּבֵּד כַּיֶּלֶק	
7	3	הִתְכַּבְּדִי כָּאַרְבֶּה	
6	2	הִרְבֵּית רֹכְלַיִךְ	16
8	3	מִכּוֹכְבֵי הַשָּׁמָיִם	
7	3	יֶלֶק פָּשַׁט וַיָּעֹף	
7	3	מִנְּזָרַיִךְ כָּאַרְבֶּה	17
9	4	וְטַפְסְרַיִךְ כְּגוֹב גֹּבָי	
11	4	הַחוֹנִים בַּגְּדֵרוֹת בְּיוֹם קָרָה	
9	4	שֶׁמֶשׁ זָרְחָה וְנוֹדְדוּ	
7	3	וְלֹא־נוֹדַע מְקוֹמוֹ	
7	3	אַיָּם נָמוּ רֹעֶיךָ	18
4	2	מֶלֶךְ אַשּׁוּר	
7	3	יִשְׁכְּנוּ אַדִּירֶיךָ	
6	2	נָפֹשׁוּ עַמְּךָ	
4	2	עַל־הֶהָרִים	
5	2	וְאֵין מְקַבֵּץ	

Translation: Nahum 3:15b-18

Multiply like the young locust,
multiply like the locust;
16 Multiply your merchants,
more than the stars of the heavens;
the young locust sheds its coat and flies away.

17 Your guards are like locusts
and your recruiting-officers like a swarm of locusts,
which settle on the walls on a cold day;
the sun rises and they go away
and their place is not known.

18 Where are your shepherds slumbering?
O King of Assyria,
Where are your nobles at rest?
Your troops expire
upon the mountains,
with none to gather them up.

Text: Nahum 3:19

Syllable Count	Stress Count	
7	3	19 אֵין־כֵהָה לְשִׁבְרֵךְ
6	2	נַחְלָה מַכָתֵךְ
7	3	כֹל שֹׁמְעֵי שִׁמְעֲךָ
7	3	תָקְעוּ כַף עָלֶיךָ
7	3	כִי עַל־מִי לֹא עָֽבְרָה
6	2	רָעָתְךָ תָמִיד

Translation: Nahum 3:19

19 There is no relief for your fracture,
your wound is severe;
All who hear news of you,
clap their hands because of you;
For over whom has not passed
your continuing evil?

Philological Commentary

3 : 1

ʿîr dāmîm : " city of blood ". Cf. Ezek. 22 : 2 ; 24 : 6,9. M. Dahood (1) believes that *dāmîm* sometimes has a double sense, " blood/ idols ", the second meaning based on *dāmāh,* " be like ".

pereq ... ṭārep : " plunder ... prey ". These two nouns are in chiastic parallelism. The collocation of *prq* and *ṭrp* is found in Ps. 7 : 3. Cognate *prq* occurs in Aramaic *AIS*, I : B : 34, [*l*]*prq wlmšlḥ yd,* " (will not be able) to destroy (it) or raise a hand against it ".

3 : 2

weqôl raʿaš ʾôpān : " And the sound of the rumbling wheel ". *qôl* denotes the noise of chariots in Joel 2 : 5, and of wheels in Ezek. 3 : 13, *qôl hāʾôpannîm,* " sound of the wheels " (followed by *weqôl raʿaš gādôl,* " sound of a great rumbling "). For the use of *raʿaš* in military contexts, cf. Is. 9 : 4 ; Jer. 47 : 3 ; Job 39 : 24. *ʾôpan* has a counterpart in Ugar. *apn*, dual *apnm*, plur. *apnt.* Note *UT*, 1121 : 1, *ṯmn mrkbt ...* (: 3) *yd apnthn,* " eight chariots with their wheels ", and compare Exod. 14 : 25, *ʾōpan markebōtāyw,* and 1 Kings 7 : 33, *ʾôpan hammerkābāh.*

wesûs dōhēr : " and galloping horse ". The root *dhr* is found in the Song of Deborah, Judg. 5 : 22, *ʾāz hālemû ʿiqqebê sûsīm dahªrôt* (MT *sûs middahªrôt*) *dahªrôt ʾabbîrāyw,* " Then loud beat the horses hooves, with the galloping, galloping of his steeds ". Albright (2) takes *dhr* (verb) as " race chariots ", and *dōhēr,* " chariot driver ", meanings which might be suitable in the Song of Deborah, but in Nahum.

ûmerkābāh meraqqēdāh : " and jolting chariot ". Note the alliteration and assonance of the phrase in the Hebrew. It is almost

(1) *Psalms I*, pp. 31-32.
(2) *BASOR* 62 (1936) 30.

impossible to do justice to the Hebrew in translation. Impressive however is the Spanish version of Nah. 3 : 2-3 by Alonso Schökel : " Ruido de látigo, ruido estruendoso de ruedas, caballo gallopando, carro rebotando ; jinetas enhiestos, fulgor de espada, relámpago de lanza, multitud de heridos, masa de cadáveres ". (3) Worthy of comparison is Joel 2 : 5, *k^{e}qôl markābôt ʿal rāʾšê hehārîm y^{e}raqqēdûn*, " With the noise of chariots, they leap on the tops of the mountains ". (4) Heb. *rāqad* ; Akk. *raqādu* ; Ar. *rqd*, = " dance, skip about ". The root has turned up in Ugaritic. *UT*, 602 : 4-5 has *rqdm*, " dancers ", and the same root is found in several Ugar. proper names. (5) H. Donner and W. Röllig (6) link the proper name *brqd*, in a Punic inscription from Ibiza, with *bʿl mrqd** which seems to underlie Greek *Balmarkōs* (*CIG* 4536) and Latin *Balmarcodi* (*CIL* III 155,3), " Dancing Baal ".

3 : 3

pārāš maʿ^{a}leh : " charging spanhorse ". *maʿ^{a}leh* is the hiphil participle of *ʿālāh*. The hiphil of *ʿālāh* is found in Jer. 51 : 27, *haʿ^{a}lû sûs*, " bring up horses ", but in Nahum, *maʿ^{a}leh* implies rather more action. Haldar has " (The horseman) spurring on ". (7) The rendering " spanhorse " for *pārāš* follows the suggestion of S. Mowinckel. (8)

pārāš maʿ^{a}leh is probably the fourth of the series of cola in verse 2. Then the syllable count for verse 2 + *pārāš maʿ^{a}leh* would be 8/4/8/5, and for verse 3, 10/9/8/8/.

w^{e}lahab ... ûb^{e}raq : " flash of ... gleam of ". *lahab*, " flash ", is sometimes used by itself to signify " blade ". Cf. Judg. 3 : 22 ; Job 39 : 23 (*lahab ḥ^{a}nît*). Note also 1 Sam. 17 : 7, *lahebet ḥ^{a}nîtô*, and (for *bārāq*) Hab. 3 : 11, *b^{e}raq ḥ^{a}nîtekā*. *bārāq*, lit. " lightning ", means " gleaming point ", in Job 20 : 25. (9)

ḥālāl ... pāger : " slain ... corpses ". Note the parallelism of *w^{e}ḥallêhem ... ûpigrêhem* in Is. 34 : 3 and the collocation *pigrê ... ḥ^{a}lālîm* in Jer. 41 : 9.

(3) *Estudios de Poëtica Hebrea*, p. 437.

(4) See the remarks of L. Alonso Schökel, *ibid.*, pp. 409-410.

(5) Cf. the observations of Dahood concerning Ps. 29 in *UHP* 72, and consult *UT*, Glossary Nos. 1274 and 2351, *Supplement*, § 19.711a.

(6) *KAI*, II, p. 89. Cf. also, Dahood, *Psalms I*, p. 178.

(7) *Studies*, p. 85.

(8) *VT* 12 (1962) 277-299.

(9) Cf. Pope, *Job*, p. 140, n. 25b.

Almost certainly related to Heb. *peger* is Ugar. *pgr*, " mortuary-offering ". Cf. *UT*, 1158 : A : 2, B : 1 ; 2006 : 2. An Akkadian letter from the Mari archives mentions a " *pagrum*-sacrifice to Dagan ", (10) which Moran (11) suggests is a kind of sacrifice associated with the cult of the dead. The Aram. cognate is clear as for example in *AIS*, I : B : 30, *wpgr 'rb' m'l pgr b'r*[*p*]*d*, " And *I shall pile* corpse upon corpse in Ar[pad] ".

lagg^{e}*wiyyāh :* " to the bodies ". The Heb. noun is in the singular, after *w*^{e}*'ên qēṣeh.* Compare sing. *latt*^{e}*kûnāh* in Nah. 2 : 10, again after *w*^{e}*'ên qēṣeh.*

The LXX once again came to grief, offering *tois éthnesin autēs* = *laggôyehā*, " to her nations ". Furthermore, the LXX attaches the first two words or so of verse 4 to the end of the present verse and arrives at the following version : *kai ouk ēn péras tois éthnesin autēs* ; *kai asthenēsousin en tois sōmasin autōn apò plēthous porneías*, " and there was no end to her nations ; but they shall be weak in their bodies because of the abundance of fornication ".

With the reference in this verse to the " mass of corpses ", this may be a good place to mention a parallel from Sumerian literature, in a text published by J. van Dijk. (12) Compare it especially with Nah. 2 : 4-3 : 3.

A l'intérieur de la ville
un massacre eut lieu,
dans les rues
les cadavres gîsaient ;
les familles se tournaient
les unes contre les autres.
Sur les parvis spacieux
le combat se déchaîna ;
on tuait au fil de l'épée.
Dans les rues
c'était la perdition. (113)

It should be mentioned that the text is describing the effects of an insurrection and not, as in Nahum, the destruction of the city by a

(10) Translation of Moran, *ANET Supplement* 623, line 50.
(11) *ANET Supplement* 623, n. 8. Cf. also, Moran's note (p. 624) on *pa-ag-ra-i.*
(12) *JCS* 19 (1965) 1-25.
(13) *Ibid.* 6.

foreign power. However, the phraseology is much the same. According to van Dijk ([14]), the style of the Sumerian text is much like that of the lamentations over the fall of cities, with a stereotyped phraseology. We shall be referring later to the " Lamentation over the Destruction of Sumer and Ur ", in the discussion of verse 18.

3:4

mērōb : " Because of the numerous ". Here we have an example of the causal force of *min*. Compare Zech. 2 : 8 *mērōb 'ādām ûbᵉhēmāh bᵉtôkāh*, " because of the multitude of men and cattle in it ".

ba'ᵃlat kᵉšāpîm : " a mistress of sorceries ". Hardly as flattering as the titles of the goddess 'Anat in *UT*, 602, *b'lt mlk*, " Mistress of Kingship " ; *b'lt drkt*, " Mistress of Dominion ", and *b'lt šmm rmm*, " Mistress of the High Heavens. ([15]) In 1 Sam. 28 : 7, the Witch of Endor is referred to as *ba'ᵃlat 'ôb*, " medium ".

hammukkeret gôyim : " Who is known by the nations ". MT *hammōkeret* has never been adequately explained. *mōkeret* would be the qal participle fem. sing. of *mākar*, " sell ". *mākar bᵉ* means " sell for ", as, for example, in Joel 4 : 3, *wᵉhayyaldāh mākᵉrû bayyayin wayyištû*, " and they have sold a girl for wine, that they might drink ". Cf. also, Amos 2 : 6, and Ps. 44 : 13. But the " harlot " in Nahum is manifestly not selling the nations for her own harlotries ! The present writer formerly explained the *beths* in *bizᵉnûnehā* and *bikᵉšāpehā* as partitive. ([16]) Thus the meaning offered was : " Who sells nations her harlotries, and clans her sorceries ". However, a new etymology for *hmkrt* has been suggested by Dahood. ([17]) He repoints MT *hammōkeret* to *hammukkeret*, the hophal fem. participle of *nkr*, the hiphil of which means " know, recognize ". He notes 2 Kings 12 : 6, *makkārô*, " his acquaintance ", and 2 Kings 12 : 8, *makkārêkem*, " your acquaintances ". He parses *gôyim* and *mišpāḥôt* as genitives of cause (Joüon, *GHB* § 121p ; GK § 116 1) and compares Is. 53 : 4, *mukkēh 'ᵉlōhîm*, " the one struck by God ", and Phoen. Karatepe, *KAI*, 26 : AI : 1, *hbrk b'l*, " the one blessed by Baal ". Therefore we have adopted Dahood's explanation and, taking the *h* of *hammukkeret*

([14]) *Ibid.* 4,14.
([15]) Cf. Albright, *Yahweh*, p. 130.
([16]) This was the position taken in my original dissertation.
([17]) " Causal *Beth* and the Root NKR in Nahum 3,4 ", *Biblica* 52 (1971) 395-396.

as a relative pronoun, translate *hammukkeret gôyīm*, " Who is known by the nations ".

D. W. Thomas [18] has attempted to establish a Heb. root *mkr*, " practise deceit, guile ", in 1 Kings 21 : 20,25, and 2 Kings 17 : 17. ZLH 435b posits the same meaning (" dolo decepit alqm ") for a root *mkr* in Nahum also. [19] 4QpNah reads *hmmkrt*.

gôyīm ... ûmišpāḥôt : " by the nations ... and by the clans ". The *mišpāḥāh*, " clan ", (= Ugar., Phoen. *špḥ*) is a subdivision of the *gôy*, " nation ", as in Ps. 22 : 28 ; 96 : 7.

3 : 5

hinᵉnî 'ēlayik : " Behold I am against you ". Here, the function of *hinnēh* is similar to that in 2 : 14.

wᵉgillêtî šûlayik ʿal pānāyik : " And I am going to lift your skirts over your face ". It is difficult to give a literal rendering of *wᵉgillêtî šûlayik*. In the piel, *glh* has the notion of " uncovering, revealing ", but it makes little sense to render like J. M. P. Smith, " I will uncover thy skirts ", [20] or, with the KJ, " I will discover thy skirts ". The *NEB* has " I will uncover your breasts to your disgrace ", which is not a translation of the Hebrew. With this verse should be compared Jer. 13 : 26, *wᵉgam 'ᵃnî ḥāśaptî šûlayik ʿal pānāyik wᵉnir'āh qᵉlônēk*, " It was I myself who snatched your skirt up over your face, exposing your shame " (J. Bright, *Jeremiah*, p. 94). The idea of " stripping ", contained in *ḥāśap*, is precisely the notion expressed be *glh* in our verse in Nahum. Bright renders Jer. 13 : 22, *nigᵉlû šûlayik*, " your limbs are exposed ", [21] and takes *šûlayik*, lit. " your skirts ", as a euphemism (cf. LXX, Vulg.) [22]. In fact, *šûl*, was rendered by the versions in similar fashion in a number of texts. Thus in Nahum,

[18] " The Root *mkr* in Hebrew ", *JTS* 37 (1936) 388-389 ; *idem*, " A Further Note on the Root *mkr* in Hebrew ", *JTS* 3 (1952) 214.

[19] Before ending the discussion of *mkr*, it should be mentioned that Ullendorff, *VT* 6 (1956) 194, on the basis of Eth. *mkr*, " to counsel ", has proposed rendering Gen. 49 : 5, *kᵉlê ḥāmās mᵉkērōtêhem*, " strong weapons are their counsels ". But compare the explanation of *mkrtyhm* as " circumcision blades ", by Dahood, *CBQ* 23 (1961) 54-56.

[20] *CECBN* 334.

[21] *Jeremiah*, p. 93.

[22] *Ibid.*, p. 95.

the LXX has *tà opísō sou,* " your backside " (?), and the Vulg. *pudenda sua* (but in Jer. 13 : 26, *femora tua*).

šûl is usually related to Ar. *sawila,* " hang down loose ".

wᵉhar'êtî : " and I will show ". Here we have an example of the hiphil perfect with original *a* in the first syllable. (23)

maʿrēk : " your nakedness ". The LXX renders it *tēn aischúnēn sou,* " your shame ".

Using this verse of Nahum as a parallel, Hillers has proposed reading in Aram. Sefîre, I : A : 40-41, [*w'yk zy tʿrr z*]*n*[*yh*] *kn yʿrrn nšy mtʿʾl wnšy ʿqrh wnšy r*[*bwh ...*], " And just as a prostitute is stripped naked, so may the wives of Matiʿʾel be stripped naked, and the wives of his offspring and the wives of his nobles ". (24) According to Hillers (25) this verse of Nahum, and Jer. 13 : 26-27 ; Ezek. 16 : 37-38 ; 23 : 10,29 ; Hos. 2 : 5, 12 are parallels to a treaty-curse concerned with the punishment of a prostitute by stripping.

3 : 6

šiqqūṣîm : " filth ". In most other places in the Old Testament where *šiqqûṣ* occurs, it usually has some relations to the detested idols of pagan worship. Cf. Deut. 29 : 16 ; 1 Kings 11 : 5,7, etc.

kᵉrō'î : " a spectacle ". *rᵒ'î* has been discussed by J. Weingreen (26) who notes Rashi's interpretation of this word in Nahum, as " excrement ". In fact Rashi's proposal was accepted by E. Sellin, and now appears in the *NEB*. R. Weiss, (27) comparing the MT and the text of 4QpNah, of this verse, regards *r'y* as a rare word, meaning " dirt, excrement ". Driver's proposal to read *kaddāʾāh,* " as a woman in menstruation ", (28) is too radical and has rightly been rejected by Haldar. (29) *rō'î* in Nahum has been compared by Lidzbarski, (30) and Cooke, (31) with Moabite *ryt,* which they derive from

(23) GK § 53 p.

(24) *Treaty-Curses*, pp. 58-60. Hillers' restorations have been accepted by Fitzmyer, *AIS*, pp. 14-15 ; 57.

(25) *Treaty-Curses*, pp. 59-60.

(26) *VT* 4 (1954) 57.

(27) *Revue de Qumran* No. 15 (1963) 437.

(28) *JTS* 41 (1940) 172-173.

(29) *Studies*, p. 68.

(30) *Handbuch der nordsemitischen Epigraphik*, p. 366.

(31) *NSI* 11.

r'h (elision of '). Smith ([32]) equates Moabite *ryt* with a form *re'iyyāh*. Lines 11-12 of the Mesha stele read: *w'lthm bqr w'ḥzh w'hrg 't kl h'm* [...] *hqr ryt lkmš wlm'b*, ([33]) which Ullendorff renders, " But I fought against the town and took it and I slew all the people of the town, a spectacle for Chemosh and Moab ". ([34]) Albright ([35]) takes Moabite *ryt* to mean " satiation " or " intoxication ".

3:7

kol rō'ayik yiddôd mimmēk : " every one who sees you will go away from you ". For the same collocation of *rō'eh* and *nādad* in a similar context, compare Ps. 31:12, *rō'ay baḥûṣ nādedû mimmennî*, " Those who see me in the street go away from me ".

šoddedāh : " is ruined ". For the form, cf. commentary on Nah. 2:4, *me'oddām*. For the nuance of *šdd* here in Nahum compare Is. 15:1 and Jer. 48:1. Jer. 48:18, *šōdēd mô'āb*, " a destroyer of Moab " is worthy of mention as also is RS 24.247 : 13, [*ml*]*kn* [*y*]*šdd ḥwt ib*, " Our King will devastate the foe's territory ". ([36])

mî yānûd lāh ... menaḥamîm lāk : " who will grieve for her ... comforters for you? " In Is. 51:19, words of cheer addressed to Jerusalem, *mî yānûd lāk* " who will grieve for you? " are balanced by *mî yenaḥamēk*, " who will comfort you? ". Notice the same collocation of roots in Job 2:11, *lānûd lô ûlenaḥamô*, " to condole with him and to comfort him ".

'abaqqēš : " will I seek ". The root is found in Heb., Phoen., and Ugar. (*bqṯ*) only.

lāk : " for you ". *lāk* is frequently emended to *lāh*, " for her ", to balance the previous *lāh*. The Wadi Murabba'ât scroll has *lk*. E. Dhorme, ([37]) commenting on this verse, observes that a sudden change of persons is characteristic of the prophetic style. The practice is also found in Northwest Semitic curses. ([38]) Dahood, ([39]) comment-

([32]) *CECBN* 356.
([33]) *KAI*, 181 : 11-12.
([34]) *Documents from Old Testament Times*, edited by D. Winton Thomas, p. 196.
([35]) *BASOR* 89 (1943) 16, n. 55.
([36]) Text published by A. Herdner, *Syria* 46 (1969) 132.
([37]) *La Bible de la Pléiade*, II, p. 799.
([38]) Cf. S. Gevirtz, *VT* 11 (1961) 147, n. 4. Dahood, *Psalms I*, pp. 35, 143.
([39]) *Psalms II*, p. 83-84.

ing on the change of persons in Ps. 61, points out the phenomenon in the Yeḥawmilk inscription (*KAI*, 10).

In this verse, note the repetition of *d : ydwd, šddh, ynwd.*

3:8

nō' 'āmôn : " No-Amon ". That is, Thebes, which was taken and sacked by the Assyrian army in 663 B.C. Amon was an Egyptian deity, and although he was the chief god of Thebes (No-Amon = " City of Amon "), in the 18th dynasty he became supreme god of the nation. (40) EA 71 : 5 and 86 : 4, two letters from Rib-Adda of Byblos, read : *dAmana ilu ša šarri bēlika tidinu baštaka ina panī šarri bēlika,* " May Amon, the god of the king your lord, establish your power in the presence of the king your lord ". (41) And from Ras Shamra comes a Ugaritic letter, addressed to the Pharaoh, and invoking the protection of Amon and other Egyptian gods for the Pharaoh : *UT*, 1018 : 20-22, *w urk ym bʿly lpn amn w l pn il mṣrm,* " And length of day for my lord in the presence of Amon and in the presence of the gods of Egypt ".

'ašer ḥêl yām mayim ḥômātāh : " whose outer-wall was the sea, water her ramparts ". The only change of pointing is *mayim* instead of MT *miyyām.* Thus *ḥêl yām* is chiastically paralled by *mayim ḥômātāh.* H. J. van Dijk would read *'ašer ḥêl yām-m yām hômātāh,* " her rampart is the Nile, the River her wall ". (42) The scroll of the Minor Prophets from Wadi Murabbaʿât has the reading *ḥyl mym* and, in fact, Haldar proposes *'ašer ḥêlê mayim ḥômātāh,* " whose wall was ramparts of water ". (43) The MT could be sustained and, recently P. R. Berger has compared it with a line from an inscription of the Assyrian king Esarhaddon :

ša dūrānūšunu tâmtumma edû šalḫûšun
deren Mauern das Meer und deren Vormauer die Wasserflut ist. (44)

(40) Cf. H. Frankfort, *Ancient Egyptian Religion*, p. 22.
(41) Translation by Moran, *Biblica* 45 (1964) 80-81.
(42) *Ezechiel's Prophecy*, p. 40.
(43) *Studies*, pp. 69-70.
(44) *Ugarit-Forschungen* 2 (1970) 346.

Berger's version of the Nahum text is: "deren Vormauer Meer war (und) aus Meer ihre Hauptmauer bestand". (45)

Ramparts were sometimes protected by an outer-wall, built some distance from the rampart. This "outer-wall" is the *ḥêl*, in contrast to the *ḥômāh*, "wall" or "rampart". (46) Note Is. 26:1, *ḥômôt wāḥēl*, and Lam. 2:8, *ḥēl wᵉḥômāh*. In the latter text, the Vulg. renders *ḥēl*, *antemurale*. There is still no agreement concerning the etymology of *ḥêl*, the most recent lexicon (*HALAT* 299a) relating it, to Ar. *ḥaul*, "what is round about", and S. Ar. *ḥwl*, "round about". It is almost certainly related to Ugar. *ḥl* (*UT*, 125:7-8), and to *ḥl* in place names (47). C. Rabin (48) rejects the connection of *ḥēl* with the abovementioned Ar. roots and takes it to be of Hittite origin: Hittite *ḫīla*, *ḫēla*, "fence, court".

The LXX rendered *ḥyl*, *archē*. Given the nuances of Gk. *archē*, it is by no means certain that the LXX translator derived *ḥyl* from *ḥll* (hiphil, "begin") as has been suggested by older critics. The Greek text of the Minor Prophets from Naḥal Ḥever has *ischùs*.

The recognition of the suffix of *ḥômātāh* as a doubleduty suffix makes the emendation *ḥêlāh*, proposed in the apparatus of *BH*³, quite superfluous. Notice that 4QpNah has *ḥylh*.

3:9

kûš ... pûṭ wᵉlûbîm : "Cush ... Put and the Libyans". Cush is sometimes equated with Ethiopia, which can be confusing since ancient Ethiopia was not the same region as modern Ethiopia, but took in the area now called Sudan. Put is more difficult to explain but seems to have been somewhere in the region of Libya. (49) A. George (50) suggests that *pûṭ* is the Punt of the ancient Egyptian texts. The land of Punt was roughly modern Somaliland. Cush and Put are mentioned together in Jer. 46:9. Regarding *lûbîm*, "Libyans", a Neo-Punic inscription from Rās el Haddāǧia, *KAI*, 118:2, mentions *lwbym*, "Libyans", (and, incidentally, the god Amon).

(45) *Ibid.* But compare the German version of H. Brunner, *AfO* 16 (1952) 262, "deren Vorwerk der Nil, deren Mauer das Wasser war", and note *BJ*, "Pour avant-mur elle avait la mer, pour rempart, les eaux".

(46) Cf. de Vaux, *Ancient Israel*, pp. 232-233.

(47) For these place names, cf. *UT*, Glossary No. 861.

(48) *Orientalia* 32 (1963) 120.

(49) Cf. the discussion in T. O. Lambdin, "Put", in *IDB*, Vol. 3, p. 971.

(50) *Michée, Sophonie, Nahum*, p. 93.

ʿoṣmāh : " her strength ". Consonantal *ʿsmḥ* probably represents *ʿōṣem* plus third fem. sing. suffix. Cf. LXX, *hē ischùs autēs*. One might take *ʿṣmh* as the noun *ʿoṣmāh* found in Is. 40 : 29 (// *kōaḥ*, " strength ") and Is. 47 : 9. In that case, the suffix of *ʿezrātēk* would also serve *ʿoṣmāh*. However, in choosing the rendering " her strength," one can explain the change of persons as representative of the phenomenon referred to in the commentary on verse 7.

beʿezrātēk : " in your army ". This version has been proposed by Dahood, (51) who derives *ʿezrātēk* from *ʿzr* II (52) = Ugar. *ǵzr*, the derived noun *ǵzr* meaning " warrior ". To support his interpretation of *beʿezrātēk*, " in your army ", Dahood points out Ezek. 27 : 10, *pāras welûd ûpûṭ hāyû beḥêlēk ʾanšê milḥamtēk*, " Persia and Lud and Put were the men of war in your army ". (53)

A comparison of this verse of Nahum with *UT*, 68 : 5 is worthwhile. The Ras Shamra text reads : *larṣ ypl ulny wl ʿpr ʿẓmny*, which Ginsberg renders : " To the earth shall fall the strong, to the dust the mighty ". (54) Gordon (55) acknowledges that Ugar. *ʿẓm* means " mighty ", but in the chapter on adverbs in *UT*, he analyses *ʿẓmny* as *ʿẓm* with an adverbial suffix *-ny*, and therefore meaning " violently ". (56) *ulny* is not easy to analyse. The *-ny*, of both *ʿẓmny* and *ulny*, may be afformative rather than adverbial. (57) *ul* signifies " army ", as in *UT*, Krt : 88, *ṣbuk ul mad*, " your troops are a mighty army ". Thus, in Nahum *ʿṣmh* is balanced by *ʿzrtk*, and in the Ugar. text, *ulny* is balanced by *ʿẓmny*. *ʿṣm* refers to military strength in such texts as Joel 2 : 5, and Dan. 11 : 25. Note also Deut. 8 : 17, *kōḥî weʿōṣem yādî*, " my power and the might of my hand ".

(51) *Psalms I*, p. 210.

(52) The presence of *ʿzr* II in Hebrew is well established. A bibliography of discussions of the root, beginning with Ginsberg, *JBL* 57 (1938) 210-211, can be found in P. D. Miller, " Ugaritic ǴZR and Hebrew ʿZR II ", *Ugarit-Forschungen* 2 (1970) 160, n. 5.

(53) *Psalms I*, p. 210.

(54) *ANET* 130.

(55) *UT*, Glossary No. 1842.

(56) *UT*, § 11.3.

(57) So *UT*, § 8.58 ; Dahood, *UHP* 16-17. However, Dahood (private communication) suggests that the suffixes of *ulny* and *ʿẓmny* may be 3rd. pers. sing. possessives.

3 : 10

gam hîʼ laggōlāh : " Yet she went into exile ". *gam* is used no fewer than four times in this and the following verse. Concerning MT, *hîʼ laggōlāh*, Ehrlich wrote : " Mann sagt hebräisch *hlk bgwlh* aber nicht *hlk lgwlh* ". (58) It is true that one normally finds *hlk bgwlh* as in Jer. 48 : 11 ; 49 : 3 ; Ezek. 12 : 11 ; 25 : 3 ; Amos 1 : 1. In fact, there is a variant reading *bgwlh* in 4QpNah. Dahood, discussing the Qumran reading, prefers the MT *laggōlāh*, but takes the *l* as an emphatic lamed with the feminine participle *gōlāh* and renders the colon : " Yet she was an exile herself ". (59) However, one cannot exclude the possibility that *l* here is a preposition, with *laggōlāh* a stylistic variant of normal *baggōlāh*, balanced by *baššebî*, " into captivity ", in the following colon. Recently Dahood has noted that in Is. 22 : 15, *lek bōʼ ʼel hassōkēn hazzeh ʻal šubnāʼ ʼašer ʻal habbāyit*, " Come now, go to this steward, to Shubna, who is over the palace ", (60) the verb *bōʼ* is used with two different prepositions. He compares Is. 7 : 4 ; 46 : 13, but especially Is. 30 : 29, *lābôʼ bᵉhar yahweh ʼel ṣûr yiśrāʼēl*, " to go to the mountain of Yahweh, to the Rock of Israel ", (60) where *lābôʼ* governs two different prepositions *bᵉ* and *ʼel*. It would be interesting research to examine texts like *UT*, 1 Aqht : 40-42, *ʻrpt tmṭr bqẓ ṭl yṭll lǧnbm*, " a cloud raining upon the summer-fruit, dew distilling upon the grapes ", to find out whether the prepositions (in this case *b/l*) are employed merely because they are the ones to be used with the respective verbs, or whether they are stylistic alternatives.

baššebî : " into captivity ". *šᵉbî* has a Ugar. counterpart in *šb*, *šby*, e.g. *UT*, 68 : 29-30, *kšbyn zb*[*l ym k*]*šbyn ṭpṭ nhr*, " For our captive is Prin[ce Yam], Our captive is Judge Nahar " (*ANET* 131). Cf. Ps. 68 : 19. In Ps. 78 : 61, *šᵉbî* has the concrete meaning " captors ". (62) Aram. *šby*, is found in Panammū II, *KAI*, 215 : 8.

ʻōlālehā yᵉruṭṭᵉšû : " Her little ones were dashed to pieces ". There is no necessity to emend *yᵉruṭṭᵉšû* to perfect *ruṭṭᵉšû*. In the light of Ugaritic, one can now perceive more clearly that the *yqtl* form could express past time, and is often balanced by a *qtl* in poetry. (63)

(58) *Randglossen*, p. 298.
(59) *Biblica* 50 (1969) 271.
(60) *Biblica* 50 (1969) 344.
(61) *Ibid.*
(62) Cf. Dahood, *Psalms II*, p. 246.
(63) Cf. Dahood, *Psalms III*, pp. 420 f.

nikbaddehā : " her nobles ". Cf. Is. 3 : 5 ; 23 : 8, where the merchants of Tyre are *nikbaddê 'āreṣ*. Heb. *nikbād* = Ugar. *nkbd* (*UT*, 1 : 2). Note that the form of the participle in the N conjugation has a prefix *n-*, a feature which is unusual in the Semitic languages and peculiar to Ugar., Heb., and Phoen. (64)

yaddû gôrāl : " they cast lots ". The same phrase is used concerning the allotting of prisoners of war in Joel 4 : 3 and Obad. 11. In Arabic, *ǧarl^{un}* means " a pebble, small stone ", which was probably used with others like a dice. (65)

rutt^{e}qû : " were bound ". This is the only occurrence of the verb, unless one accepts the Q *yrtq*, in Eccles. 12 : 6 for the K *yrḥq*. The meaning is certain in view of the derivatives *rattîqāh*, " chain ". (1 Kings 6 : 21), and *r^{e}tūqôt*, " chains " (Is. 40 : 19).

bazziqqîm : " in chains ". The same word is used in Ps. 149 :8,

le'sōr malkêhem b^{e}ziqqîm
w^{e}nikb^{e}dêhem b^{e}kablê barzel
To bind their kings with chains
and their nobles with fetters of iron.

Note the play on the consonants in the second half of verse 10 : *d* in *w^{e}'al nikbaddehā yaddû gôrāl*, and *q* in *w^{e}kol g^{e}dôleha rutt^{e}qû bazziqqîm*.

3 : 11

tiśśāk^{e}rî : " you will hire yourself out ". Driver (66) following Duhm, prefers to read *tiśśāk^{e}rî*, " you will hire yourself out ", for MT, *tišk^{e}rî*, " you will become drunk ". Gaster (67) and Dahood (68) accept the same reading, but point for further support to *UT*, Krt : 97-98, *almnt škr tškr*, " the widow hires herself out ". See now *NEB*.

t^{e}hî na'^{a}lāmāh : " you will become young again ". *na'^{a}lāmāh* is difficult. Traditionally, it has been taken as a form of *'lm*, " conceal,

(64) Cf. Moscati, *An Introduction to the Comparative Grammar of the Semitic Languages*, § 16.99.

(65) Consult J. Lindblom, " Lot-casting in the Old Testament ", *VT* 12 (1962) 164-178. I have not been able to see the Theology Dissertation of E. Renner, *A Study of the Word gôral* (Heidelberg 1958).

(66) *JTS* 39 (1938) 271.

(67) *JTS* 38 (1937) 164.

(68) *CBQ* 17 (1955) 104.

hide ", and thus " be ignorant, obscured ". (69) Driver proposes *naʿ^{a}lāmāh*, " must become worn with toil ". (70) Gaster reads *l^{e}ʿalmāh*, " (become) a serving-maid ". (71) Dahood, respecting both the consonantal text and the Massoretic vocalisation, renders *t^{e}hî naʿ^{a}lāmāh*, " you will be made young again ". (72) This suggestion has been accepted here. *naʿ^{a}lāmāh* should be related then to Heb. *ʿalmāh*, Ugar. *ǵlmt*, Phoen. *ʿlmt*, " young maiden, young woman " ; Aram. (Palmyrene), *ʿlymtʾ*, " harlots ". (73) Dahood notes that Syr. *ʿallēm* means " to renew ones youth ". (74) It would be interesting to know how the *NEB* obtains " flaunting your sex " !

An alternative solution has been proposed to the writer by Dahood (private communication). It consists of reading *tihyennā(h) ʿalmāh*, and explaining the verb as the energic mood. The meaning is not affected, but the reading has the merit of not requiring any explanation for an unusual word.

Hillers (75) has investigated the Semitic curse of becoming a harlot. He quotes, for example, the curse in the Ashurnirari Treaty : " Then may the aforesaid indeed become a prostitute, and his warriors women ". (76) Nahum refers to warriors becoming women in v. 13 below.

3 : 12

mibṣārayik : " your fortifications ". Related to *mibṣār* is the verb *bṣr*, found twice in the piel, Is. 22 : 10 and Jer. 51 : 53. Possibly, the root is a cognate of Ugar. *bṣr*, which Gordon takes to mean " soar ".(77) In Jer. 51 : 53, *kî taʿ^{a}leh bābel haššāmayim w^{e}kî t^{e}baṣṣēr m^{e}rôm ʿuzzāh*, " Though Babylon should mount up to heaven, and though she should raise the height of her fortress ", perhaps one can detect the notion that fortifying involves raising defences higher, and therefore Gordon's

(69) BDB 761a, " mayest thou be obscured " ; ZHL 603a, " ignorata, despecta ".
(70) *JTS* 39 (1938) 271.
(71) *JTS* 38 (1937) 164.
(72) *CBQ* 17 (1955) 104.
(73) *DISO* 214.
(74) *CBQ* 17 (1955) 104.
(75) *Treaty-Curses*, p. 58.
(76) *Ibid.*
(77) *UT*, Glossary No. 500. *HALAT* 142b follows Gordon, *contra* G. R. Driver, *CML* 164a and J. Aistleitner, *WuS* No. 564. But see also Dahood, *Psalms II*, p. 221, n. 13 ; *idem*, *UHP* 53.

definition of *bṣr*, " soar ", may be substantiated further. Bright's version, " seal off ", [78] would then be inaccurate.

A. Parrot [79] suggests that " fortresses " refers to Ashur and Tarbiṣu, the latter town being not too far from Nineveh and falling to the enemy before Nineveh. [80]

tᵉ'ēnîm : " fig-trees ". KB, 1016a, may well be right in relating Ugar. *tyt*, to Heb. *tᵉ'ēnāh*, Akk. *tittu*, " fig-tree, fig ". [81] *UT*, 12 + 97 : 13-15, although fragmentary, lists *š'rm*, *tyt*, *nbt*, and *šmn*, just as Deut. 8 : 8, lists *śᵉ'ōrāh*, " barley ", *tᵉ'ēnāh*, " fig(s) ", *šemen*, " oil ", and *dᵉbaš*, " honey ". (Ugar. *nbt* = " honey ").

'am : " your troops ". Following an impressive number of scholars, who have taken consonantal *'m* as a parallel to *mibṣārayik*, we read *'am* for MT *'im*. But we do not go as far as Smith, who comments that the MT " is lacking in parallelism " [82] and " yields too short a line ". [83] With Nowack, Marti and others, Smith emends MT *'im* to *'ammēk*, " your defenders ". [84] But *'am* is served by the double-duty suffix of *mibṣārayik*, and to emend *'am* to *'ammēk* would spoil the syllable count of a finely structured verse : the syllable count is 8/4/8/4 and the stress, 3/2/3/2.

Although we have followed the majority of scholars, taking *'m* as parallel to *mibṣārayik*, we are not absolutely convinced that parallelism must be established in this verse. *'im bikkûrîm* may not have to be a parallel to *kol mibṣārayik tᵉ'ēnîm*, for in the following cola *'al pî 'ôkēl* certainly does not parallel *'im yinnô'û wᵉnāpᵉlû*.

(78) Jeremiah, p. 352.

(79) *Nineveh and the Old Testament* p. 79.

(80) The Babylonian Chronicle reads :

(*āl*) *tar-bi-ṣu ālu šá pi-ḫat ninua*(*KI*) *i*[*ṣ-ṣ*]*ab-tu*[

They captured the town of Tarbiṣu, a city in the province of Nineveh ...

[*kišād* (*nār*)*i-d*]*iq-lat irdi-ma ina muḫḫi aššur*(*KI*) *it-ta-di ṣal-tú ana libbi āli epuš-ma*

he pursued [down the bank of the river] Tigris and encamped against Assur. He made an attack upon the town ...

(Text and translation from D. J. Wiseman, *Chronicles of Chaldaean Kings* [626-556 *B.C.*] *in the British Museum*, pp. 56-57 ; lines 25-26 of B. M. 21901).

(81) *DISO* 323 lists Jud. Aram. *t'ny'*.

(82) *CECBN* 346.

(83) *Ibid.*

(84) *Ibid.* 357.

'al pî 'ôkel : " into the mouth of the eater ". The simile of the early ripe fig falling into the mouth of the eater is found in Is. 28 : 4. One can only compare that text of course, if it is taken as symbolising how easily Samaria is taken. ([85])

The opposite of *'al pî 'ôkel.* is *UT*, 608 : 10,20, *lp akl* " from the mouth of the eater ".

3 : 13

'ammēk : " your troops ". As in the previous verse, *'am* probably signifies " troops " in this context. Compare Joel 2 : 5, *ke'am 'āṣûm 'erûk milḥāmāh,* " like a mighty army drawn up for battle ". The *NEB* understands *'ammēk,* as referring to troops, but inaccurately renders it " the troops " instead of " your troops ".

nāšîm beqirbēk : " are women in your midst ". Compare Is. 19 : 16 and Jer. 50 : 37. Hillers ([86]) has compared these texts to Ancient Near Eastern treaty-curses. For example, the Ashurnirari treaty contains this curse : " May his warriors become women " ; ([87]) and the Hittite Soldier's Oath contains the phrase : " Let them change his troops into women ". ([88]) Driver, expelling *'ammēk* from the text of Nahum " as a misplaced correction of *'im* in v. 12 (Marti) " ([89]) misses the point completely and ends up with " lo ! the women in thy midst (are fallen) to thine enemies ". ([90]) *le'ōyebayik* should be taken with what follows it, not with what goes before it.

pātôaḥ niptehû : " are opened, opened wide ". Although *niptehû* is niphal, *pātôaḥ* is the qal infinitive absolute. This is normal in Hebrew. Compare Job 6 : 2, *lû šāqôl yiššāqēl ka'śî,* " Could my anguish but be weighed " (Pope, *Job*, p. 48).

ša'arê 'arṣēk : " the gates of your city ". Heb. *ša'ar* (= Ugar. *ṯġr*, EA 244 : 16, *šaḫru*) is taken here in its usual meaning " gate ". Bright([91]) however points out that *ša'ar* could signify (*pars pro toto*) a " city ", or " town ". He renders Jer. 15 : 7, *beša'arê hā'āreṣ,* " in

(85) See for example, E. J. Kissane, *The Book of Isaiah,* I p. 315.
(86) *Treaty-Curses*, pp. 66-68.
(87) *Ibid.* p. 66.
(88) *Ibid.* p. 67.
(89) *JTS* 39 (1938) 271.
(90) *Ibid.*
(91) *Jeremiah*, p. 100, n. 2.

the outlying towns ". [92] Hence some scholars (e.g. Smith) [93] may be right in taking *šaʿarê 'arṣēk* in Nahum as referring to forts protecting the country's borders, or the outer defenses of Nineveh. In the commentary on Nah. 3 : 12, *mibṣārayik*, we referred to line 25 of the Babylonian Chronicle : " Tarbiṣu, a city in the province of Nineveh ". It could be then that *šaʿarê* refers to towns like Tarbiṣu, and that *'arṣēk* means " your land ". However we have preferred to render *šaʿarê 'arṣēk*, " the gates of your city ". *'ereṣ* can mean " city, metropolis ". [94] Cf. Akk. *erṣetu*, " quarter of a city ". [95] Note that Jerome, in his commentary on Nahum, having rendered the Hebrew " inimicis tuis adapertione pandentur portae terrae tuae ; devorabit ignis vectes tuos ", [96] comments : " Pandentur ergo portae tuae, et patebit civitas hostibus, robustissimos vectes quibus claudebantur portae, consumet ignis ". [97] Furthermore, though Jerome had no doubt that Nineveh was a city, he felt he had to say : " Portae itaque terrae Ninivae ". [98]

'ākelāh 'ēš berîḥāyik : " fire consumes your bars ". With biblical *'ākelāh 'ēš* (also Nah. 3 : 15, *tō'kelēk 'ēš*, " fire will devour you "), compare *UT*, 51 : VI : 24-25,27,29-30, *tikl išt bbhtm*, " fire consumes the houses ", and Phoen. Kilamuwa *KAI*, 24 : 6-7, which twice has the phrase *km'š 'klt*, " like a fire that consumes ". Note also Akk. *išātum mātam īkal*, " fire will devastate the country ". [99]

Heb. *berîaḥ* has a cognate in Ugar. *brḥ*. Although the contexts are quite different, *'ārṣēk/berîḥāyik* of Nahum recall *UT*, 1001 : rev. 8, *brḥ arṣ*, " gates (or bars) of the nether-city ", which compares with Jon. 2 : 7 *yāradtî hā'āreṣ berīḥehā baʿadî leʿôlām*, " I went down into the nether-city, its bars closing over me forever ".

(92) *Ibid.*, p. 105. Also note on p. 108.

(93) *CECBN* 347.

(94) Cf. Dahood, *PNWSP* 62-63 ; *idem*, *Biblica* 44 (1963) 297-298 ; 47 (1966) 280 ; van Dijk, *Ezechiel's Prophecy*, p. 53 ; Cathcart, *Biblica* 49 (1968) 513. N. Tromp, *Primitive Conceptions*, pp. 31 ff.

(95) *CAD* [E] 312.

(96) PL 25, 1264.

(97) *Ibid.*

(98) *Ibid.* 1267.

(99) *CAD* [A] I 254.

3 : 14

ša'ᵃbî : " draw ". Heb. *šā'ab*, Ugar. *š'b*, Akk. *sa'ābu*, mean specifically to " draw water " mainly for drinking purposes. [100] In *UT*, Krt : 113, *š'b* is found in the description of a siege.

Notice the chiastic arrangement of :

mê māṣôr ša'ᵃbî lāk
ḥazzᵉqî mibṣārāyik

bō'î baṭṭîṭ wᵉrimᵉsî baḥōmer : " Go into the brick-clay, and tread the mortar ". The same two pairs of words in parallelism occur in Is. 41 : 25, *wᵉyābō' sᵉgānîm kᵉmô ḥōmer ûkᵉmô yôṣēr yirmos ṭîṭ*, " And he will walk over the princes as if they were mortar, and as the potter treads brick-clay ". *bō'î* in Nahum and *wᵉyābō'* in the Isaiah text have frequently been emended to *bûsî*, " trample ", and *wayyābos*, " and he will trample ", respectively. [101] In support of these emendations, scholars call on Zech. 10 : 5, *wᵉhāyû kᵉgibbōrîm bôsîm bᵉṭîṭ ḥûṣôt bammilḥāmāh*, " and they shall be like mighty men in battle, trampling the mud of the streets ". But it is difficult to believe that the same confusion between *bw'* and *bws* would occur twice. On the contrary, the pair *bw'* // *rms* can be convincingly supported. In Mic. 5 : 4 and Phoen. Arslan Tash, *KAI*, 27 : 5-8 is the pair *bw'* // *drk*. [102] The pair *drk*//*rms* occurs in Is. 63 : 3 and Ps. 91 : 13. The MT is quite sound and there is no reason to emend *bō'î*.

In Nahum, as in Is. 41 : 25, *ṭîṭ* (= Ugar. *ṭṭ*, [103] Akk. *ṭīṭu*, *ṭiṭṭu*) signifies specifically clay for making bricks etc. In other contexts (e.g. Zech. 9 : 3 ; Ps. 18 : 43), it means " mud ".

ḥōmer means " mortar " or " clay ". KB 312b defines it as " reddish clay ", and derives it from the root *ḥmr*, " be red " (cf. Job 16 : 6) ; Ar. *ḥmr*, " be red ", *ḥumrāt*, " redness ". [104] Dahood on the other hand, connects *ḥōmer* with Ugar. *ḫmr*, which he defines as " winebowl, vat ". [105] The LXX translator, who offers *achúrois*,

(100) According to Lambdin, *Orientalia* 22 (1953) 368, El Amarna *šu-i-ib-da* represents Egyptian *šwbty*, which was originally Canaanite. Cf. also, Albright, *BASOR* 63 (1936) 30, n. 49.

(101) Most recently *HALAT* 109b, 111a ; J. L. McKenzie, *Second Isaiah*, p. 33.

(102) Cf. Cathcart, *Biblica* 49 (1968) 512.

(103) Cf. Astour, *JAOS* 86 (1966) 278 ; *Ugaritica* V, p. 578.

(104) Cf. also, *HALAT* 317a.

(105) *Biblica* 45 (1964) 408-409 ; *Psalms II*, p. 214.

" chaff-heaps " (?), seems to have been thinking of chaff or straw with clay to make bricks. Lastly, note Akk. *emēru*, " pile of bricks ". [106]

haḥ^a^zîqî malbēn : " take hold of the brick-mould ". Held [107] sees a possible parallel to *haḥ^a^zîqî malbēn* in *UT* 51 : IV : 60, *aḫd ulṯ*. He points out texts (e.g. Exod. 4 : 4), where *'ḥz* parallels *hḥzq*, and notes *mḥzyq byd* in Is. 51 : 18, which he equates with Ugar. *aḫd yd.* [108] However the meaning of Ugar. *ulṯ* is still unclear. Albright translates Ugar. *aḫd ulṯ*, " An apprentice carpenter ", [109] comparing *aḫd* to Akk. *āḫizu*, " learner ", and *ulṯ* to the foreign loanword Ilš, name of the carpenter god in Ugaritic. *malbēn* only occurs twice elsewhere, 2 Sam. 12 : 31 and Jer. 43 : 9. Its meaning in the latter text is not very clear. *lāban* = " make bricks " (Gen. 11 : 3 ; Exod. 5 : 7,14). Held [110] notes Ugar. *lbn lbnt*, " make bricks ", Akk. *libitta labānu*, Heb. *lbn lbnym*. The opposition of G. C. O'Cellaigh [111] to the translation of *malbēn* by " brick-mould " is not balanced by any constructive alternative.

3 : 15

šām : " Behold ". Analyzing *šām* as the equivalent of El Amarna *šumma*, " behold ", as it is in other texts studied by Moran [112] and Dahood. [113] Even the conservative W. Maier [114] sees that *šām* is not to be taken here as demonstrative " there ".

tō'k^e^lēk ... tō'k^e^lēk : " will devour ... will devour ". The poetic use of the same word in the first and third cola forms what Dahood has called an " A + B + A word order ". [115] Among the Ugaritic and

(106) *CAD* [E] 148.
(107) *Eretz-Israel* 9 (1969) 72, n. 17.
(108) *Ibid.*
(109) *Yahweh*, p. 122.
(110) *JBL* 84 (1965) 277, n. 25. Reference to *Enūma eliš* VI lines 60-61, *libittašu iltabnu*, " they moulded its bricks ".
(111) " And *So* David did to *all the cities* of Amon ", *VT* 12 (1962) 183.
(112) *JCS* 7 (1953) 78-80.
(113) *Biblica* 38 (1957) 306-309. *Psalms I*, pp. 81, 224, 291 ; *Psalms II*, p. 121. Cf. also, A. Jirku, *FuF* 32 (1958) 212a. Recently, J. Holman, *BZ* 14 (1970) 51, has pointed out the parallelism of *šām 'attāh*, " you are there ", and *hinn^e^kā*, " look you are there ", in Ps. 139 : 8. He compares *UT*, 95 : 10, 14, *hnny* // *ṯmny*. Yet *šām* also implies " Behold " in Ps. 139 : 8.
(114) *The Book of Nahum : A Commentary*, p. 346.
(115) *Ugarit-Forschungen* 1 (1969) 32-34.

Hebrew examples listed by Dahood, one can mention *UT*, 67 : VI : 20-22, *yṯlṯ qn ḏrʿh yḥrṯ kgn aplb kʿmq yṯlṯ bmt*, " He harrows his forearms, he plows his chest like a garden, like a valley he harrows his back " ; (116) and Ps. 104 : 15, *weyayin yeśammaḥ lebab ʾenôš lehaṣhîl pānîm miššāmen weleḥem lebab ʾenôš yisʿād*, " And with wine He gladdens the heart of man, making his face shine with oil, and with bread sustains the heart of man ". (117)

On *tōʾkelēk ʾēš*, cf. the commentary on verse 13. One could take *ʾēš* as the subject of *tōʾkelēk kayyāleq* in the third colon, but *ḥereb* in the second colon could also be the subject. Cf. Deut. 32 : 42, *weḥarbî tōʾkal bāśār*, " and my sword shall devour flesh " and Nah. 2 : 14. In the treaties of Esarhaddon one finds the phrase GÍR. MEŠ *li-ku-la-šú*, " may daggers devour him ". (118) The parallelism of *ʾēš* and *ḥereb* compares with that in *UT*, 49 : II : 30-33, *tiḫd bn ilm mt bḥrb tbqʿnn bḫṯr tdrynn bišt tšrpnn*,

> She seized the godly Mot —
> With a sword she doth cleave him.
> With fan she doth winnow him
> With fire she doth burn him. (*ANET* 140)

Thus biblical *ʾēš*//*ḥereb* corresponds to Ugar. *ḥrb* // *išt*. Note the collocation in *UT*, 137 : 32, *išt ištm yitmr ḥrb lṭšt*, " A fire, two fires ! he sees a sharpened sword ".

hitkabbedī ... hitkabbedî : " Multiply ... multiply ". The first *hitkabbedī* is written defectively, and is an imperative fem. sing. However, it could be an infinitive absolute, *hitkabbēd*, used as an imperative. See the comments on Nah. 2 : 2.

kayyeleq ... kaʾarbeh : " like the young locust ... like the locust ". Lexicographers differ in their definitions of the various terms for locusts Some modern versions (e.g. *RSV*) take *yeleq* as " locust ", and *ʾarbeh* as " grasshopper ". Both words probably mean " locust ". KB 383b defines *yeleq* as the " creeping, unwinged phase of the locust " !

The comparison of a multitude to locusts is common in ancient Near Eastern literature. Noteworthy texts are Jer. 51 : 14, *kî ʾim millēʾtîk ʾādām kayyeleq*, " Ah, I'll fill you with men as with locusts " ;(119) Jer. 51 : 27, *haʿalû sûs keyeleq sāmār*, " Bring up the horses like bristly

(116) *Ibid.*
(117) *Ibid.*
(118) *CAD* [A] I 254b.
(119) Bright, *Jeremiah*, p. 347.

ocusts ". (120) Speaking of the Babylonians who are to conquer Egypt, Jer. 46 : 23 says : *kî rabbû mē'arbeh w^e'ên lāhem mispār*, " More numerous are they than locusts, / Beyond all count ". (121) In Ugaritic one can mention Krt : 103-105, *kirby tškn šd km ḥsn pat mdbr*, " Like the locusts that dwell on the steppe, like the grasshoppers on the borders of the desert " ; ʿnt : II : 9-10, *tḥth kkdrt ri* [*š*] *ʿlh kirbym kp*, " Beneath her were heads like balls, above her, hands like locusts ". In the Sumerian " Curse of Agade ", it is related how the angry Enlil, enraged by the destruction of his beloved Ekur, avenges it by bringing down the Gutians from the mountains, " In vast numbers, like locusts, they covered the earth ..." (122) Akkadian literature provides numerous examples. From Ashurbanipal comes this statement : *sīsê imērē alpē u ṣēnē ša eli aribē* ($BURU_5$.ḪI.A) *ma'du ašlula ana Aššur*, " as booty, I carried off to Assyria horses, mules, asses, oxen and sheep, more numerous than locusts " ; (123) and from Sennacherib, *kīma tibūt aribi ma'di ša pān šatti mitḫariš ana epēš tuqmāte tebûni ṣēru'a*, " one and all, they were risen against me to offer battle, like a spring invasion of countless locusts ". (124) Egyptian texts compare defeated armies with insects.

3 : 16

hirbêt : " Multiply ". Parsing *hirbêt* as a precative or optative perfect, linked with the two imperatives in verse 15. This obviates the almost universal practice of emending *hirbêt* to imperative *harbî* (cf. *BH*[3]). The *NEB* renders it awkwardly, " you have (spies) as numerous as ". The need to recognise this usage of the precative perfect in Hebrew (as in Ugaritic, Phoenician, Aramaic, and Arabic) has been stressed by Dahood, (125) especially in translating the psalms. A good example to illustrate the usage is Ps. 4 : 2, *b^eqor'î ʿ^anēnî '^elōhê ṣidqî baṣṣār hirḥabtā lî ḥonnēnî ûš^emaʿ t^epillātî*, " When I call, answer me, O God of my vindication in distress, set me at large ; Have pity on me and hear my prayer ". (126) Here *hirḥabtā* is to be parsed as a precative perfect — it is parallel to two imperatives.

(120) *Ibid.*, p. 349.
(121) *Ibid.*, p. 304.
(122) *ANET Supplement* 649, line 157.
(123) *CAD* [E] 256.
(124) *Ibid.*
(125) Note especially *Psalms I*, p. xxxix ; *Psalms III*, pp. 415-417 ; *UHP* 38. Dahood points out Buttenweiser's efforts to bring out the use of the precative perfect in the psalms.
(126) Dahood, *Psalms I*, pp. 22-23. Cf. also, *idem*, *Commentary* 46 (September 1968) 24.

rōk^e^layik : " your merchants ". In Ezek 17 : 4, *way^e^bî'ēhû 'el 'ereṣ k^e^na'an*, " And he brought it to a land of trade ", is balanced by *b^e^'îr rōk^e^lîm śāmô*, " and set it in a city of merchants " S. Ar. *rkl* means " to go about as a trader ". The *NEB* offers " spies ".

mikkôk^e^bê haššāmayim : " more than the stars of the heavens ". This comparison reminds one of the simile in Gen. 26 : 4, *w^e^hirbêtî 'et zar'^a^kā k^e^kôk^e^bê haššāmayim*, " And I will multiply your seed like the stars of the heavens ". Cf. also Gen. 22 : 17 ; Deut. 1 : 10 ; 10 : 22. The same simile has been pointed out by Held in an Old Babylonian dialogue, three lines of which read : *e-ra-da-ni-im* (text *-ši*) *aš-šum qí-pa-a-ku ra-i-mi da-bi-ba-tu-ja e-li ka-ka-ab ša-me-e ma-da* ; " They come down to me because I (still) trust my lover, my gossipy women, more numerous than the stars of heaven ". (127) Thus, *ka-ka-ab ša-me-e* = Heb. *kôk^e^bê haššāmayim*. (128)

pāšaṭ : " sheds its coat ". This is something of a paraphrase. *pāšaṭ* means " strip off, undress ". (129) The young locust loses the outer coat it had as a larva. The significance of this whole colon and its position in the text are difficult to assess.

3 : 17

manzārayik : " Your guards ". KB follows N. Torczyner, (130) who reads *manzāzayik*, making it a cognate of Akk. *manzāzu*, " garrison, guardsman ". Torczyner rejects the association of *mnzryk* with Akk. *manṣāru*, *maṣṣāru*, " guard ". He calls for " a frequent Accadic name for a high official ", (131) corresponding to *ṭupšarru*. He points to *manzāz ekalli* and *manzāz babi* to support his *manzāzayik*. But one can indicate *maṣṣār bābāt ekalli* and *maṣṣār ekalli* also. (132) However, Akk. *manṣāru* belongs to a root *nṣr*, which ought to be *ṣ*, not *z*, in Hebrew. Perhaps a loan-word does not always develop according to the rule. The *NEB* takes *mnzryk* to mean " your secret agents " !

w^e^ṭaps^e^rayik : " and your recruiting-officers ". Literally : " scribes ". *ṭipsār* = Akk. *ṭupšarru* (Sum. *DUB.SAR*), " tablet-writer,

(127) *JCS* 15 (1961) 9, 24.
(128) Heb. *kōkāb* = Ugar. *kbkb*, Meḫri, *kbkb*. There is an alternative form in Ugar. *kkbm*. Cf. *UT*, Glossary No. 1189.
(129) Cf. GB 664b ; KB 784b.
(130) *JPOS* 16 (1936) 7.
(131) *Ibid.*
(132) Von Soden, *AHw* 621.

scribe". It is found only once elsewhere in the O. T., viz. Jer. 51 : 27, where the "recruiting-officers" [133] are mentioned together with locusts also. According to R. de Vaux, [134] the *ṭipsār* would be the "recruiting-officer", the official in charge of conscription known usually in Heb. as the *sōpēr* (2 Kings 25 : 19) or *šōṭēr* (Deut. 20 : 5-8). The ancient versions did not understand this military term borrowed from the Assyrians and Babylonians. In Nahum, the LXX has *ho súmmiktós sou,* "your companion" (?), and the Vulg. *parvuli tui,* seemingly relating the first syllable of *ṭpsr* to *ṭap*, "child". In Jer. 51 : 27 (LXX 28 : 27), the LXX rendered the term *belostáseis,* "siegeworks", and the Vulg. offers a proper name *Taphsar* !

keгôb gōbāy : "like a swarm of locusts". The phrase is quite problematical. *gōbay* means "locusts" (cf. Amos 7 : 1), but the significance of *gôb* is not clear. The traditional treatment (found even in the recent lexicon, *HALAT* 174b) is to regard *gôb* as dittography of the following *gōbāy*. W. Maier [135] (with a claim for support from GK) takes it as an example of repetition to indicate number. ZLH 145a relates *gōbay* to Ar. *ǧāba*, "permigravit". Perhaps *gôb*, if it is a genuine word, is related to the same root. But our rendering, "like a swarm of locusts", is little more than a guess.

Bearing on *gōbay* is a Heb. inscription of the 8th-7th centuries B.C., published by N. Avigad. [136] The seal inscription reads : *lʿzry w hgbh*, and underneath is represented the figure of a locust leaving no doubt that *hgbh* means "the locust". Avigad offers two explanations for the form *hgbh.* Either it is an unknown variant of biblical *gōbay*, the last syllable being contracted from the diphthong (*gōbeh* from *gōbay*, like *śādeh* from *śāday*), or it is the singular of the plural *gēbîm*, "locusts", found in Is. 33 : 4. [137] Note the alternatives in Ugaritic, *brkt* and *brky.* In the seal, *hgbh* is a proper name and therefore scholars should perhaps be on their guard against emending Neh. 11 : 8, *gabbay sallāy*, "Gabbai, Sallai", to *gibbōrê ḥayil*, "men of valour". [138] J. M. Myers [139] may well be right in taking *gby* as a proper name. Note also the Ugar. personal names *gby* and *sly.* [140]

[133] Bright, *Jeremiah*, p. 357, renders *tipṣār*, "marshalls".

[134] *Ancient Israel*, p. 251.

[135] *The Book of Nahum*, p. 355.

[136] *IEJ* 16 (1966) 50-53.

[137] Cf. KB 164b, where *gbh* is proposed as a sing. of *gēbîm.* Also *HALAT* 163b.

[138] Most recently, *HALAT* 166a has put forward this emendation.

[139] *Ezra Nehemiah*, p. 184.

[140] *UT*, Glossary, Nos. 550 and 1759.

bagg^e^dērôt : " on the walls ". Ugar. *gdrt* may well be a cognate of Heb. *g^e^dērāh,* which could refer to a " fence " or " hedge ", as well as " wall ". (141)

zār^e^ḥāh : " rises ". *zāraḥ* means " beam, shine forth, rise (of the sun) " ; *mizrāḥ,* " rising (of the sun), east ". Ullendorff (142) seems to be correct so far when he states that Heb. *zrḥ* has no equivalent in any Semitic language except Arabic. Notice that Mal. 1 : 11, *kî mimmizraḥ šemeš w^eʿad m^ebô'ô,* " For from the rising of the sun to its setting ", has a parallel in Phoen. Karatepe, *KAI,* 26 : AI : 4-5, *lmmṣ' šmš wʿd mb'y.* Note also *UT,* ʿnt : II : 8, *ṣat špš,* " sunrise ". But Hebrew also employs *yṣ'* in this sense : Gen. 19 : 23, *haššemeš yāṣā',* and Judg. 5 : 31, *k^eṣē't haššemeš.*

m^eqômô : " their place ". The suffix is mysterious. Possibly it refers back to *gôb,* " swarm ". Haldar (143) thinks that the *-ô* is an example of a modified form of the archaic nominative ending *û.*

3 : 18

'ayyām : " Where ". Heb. *'ay,* Ugar. *iy,* Akk. *ai,* is found in El Amarna as *a-ya-mi.* *'ym* here in Nahum may represent an alternative form to *'y.* *'ayyām* could represent *'ay* + 3rd masc. plur. suffix, which might be explained as prospective. We prefer the first explanation.

rōʿekā : " your shepherds ". *rōʿeh* is often used figuratively of a ruler. (144)

melek 'aššûr : " O King of Assyria ". This phrase, labelled by Kraeling as " metrically superfluous " (145) and " glossatory ", (146) is a vocative suspended between two cola. Thus, there is a 7/4/7 syllable

(141) Cf. J. B. Pritchard, *Hebrew Inscriptions and Stamps from Gibeon,* pp. 9-10. See further the review of Pritchard's work by H. Michaud in *VT* 10 (1960) 103 ; and Dahood, *Psalms II,* p. 259. A. Demsky, *BASOR* 202 (1971) 20-22 has recently discussed the problematic Heb. pers. names on the jar handles from Gibeon.

(142) *VT* 6 (1956) 196.

(143) *Studies,* p. 75. On *b^e^nô b^eʿ^ōr* (Num. 24 : 3,15) = older *binu baʿari,* consult Albright, *CBQ* 7 (1945) 22 ; *idem, Yahweh,* p. 11.

(144) KB 898 f.

(145) *Commentary on the Prophets,* Vol. II, p. 241.

(146) *Ibid.*

count and a 3/2/3 stress count. This group of cola goes with the next group, which has a 6/4/5 syllable and a 2/2/2 stress count.

yišk^enû : " are at rest ". The widely accepted emendation of *yišk^enû* to *yēš^enû*, found in the apparatus of *BH*³ is based on the common parallelism or collocation of the roots *nwm* and *yšn*, found in Is. 5 : 27 ; Ps. 76 : 6 ; 121 : 4 ; 132 : 4 ; Prov. 6 : 4,10 ; 24 : 33. The same parallelism is found in *UT*, Krt : 31-32, *bm bkyh wyšn bdmʿh nhmmt*, " As he weeps, there is sleep, as he sheds tears, slumber " ; and *UT*, Krt : 33-34, *šnt tluan wyškb nhmmt wyqmṣ*, " Sleep overcomes him and he reclines, slumber and he curls up ". However, in the light of Is. 26 : 19 and Ps. 94 : 17, *šākan* can have the notion of " (the body) reposing in death ", or even of " being entombed ". In Is. 22 : 16 and Ps. 49 : 12, *miškān* refers to the resting-place of the dead, namely the " tomb ". [147] Note *miškān* parallel to *qibrô* in Is. 22 : 16. Ar. *sakana*, can mean " be quiet, at peace ", as well as " dwell ".

nipp^ešû : " expire ". Repoint MT *nāpōšû* to *nipp^ešû*, the piel privative of *npš*, as has been suggested by Dahood. [148] In the niphal, *npš* means " take breath, refresh oneself ".

ʿamm^ekā : " Your troops ". As in verse 13, though " your people " might be right here.

w^e'ên m^eqabbēṣ : " with none to gather them up ". Probably to gather them up for burial. Lack of burial was regarded as a calamity in the ancient Near East, and the curse of no burial is frequent in ancient Near Eastern texts as Hillers [149] has shown. Dahood gives an example of the West Semitic curse from Phoen. Eshmunazor, *KAI*, 14 : 8, *w'l yqbr bqbr*, " Nor may they be buried in a grave ". [150]

This verse deserves comparison with the following lines from the " Lamentation over the Destruction of Sumer and Ur ", as translated by S. N. Kramer :

> Ur, like a single reed drops (its) head, is helpless,
> Its people, like fish caught by hand — their life is departed,
> Its lowly (and) noble lie spread about, none can rise
> For its king there was no bread to eat in the *lofty* Dubla, ...
> (*ANET Supplement* 616, lines 301-304).

(147) Cf. Dahood, *Psalms I*, pp. 298 f., *idem*, *Psalms II*, p. 138 ; W. Maier, *The Book of Nahum*, p. 360 ; Tromp, *Primitive Conceptions*, p. 32.

(148) *Psalms I*, p. 61.

(149) *Treaty-Curses*, pp. 68-69.

(150) *Psalms II*, p. 251.

kēhāh : " relief ". The apparatus of *BH*[3] indicates the doubt about the word *kēhāh.* Thus in the apparatus for the text of Nahum, it is proposed that one reads *gēhāh,* but at Prov. 17 : 22, Nah. 3 : 19 is referred to as basis for reading *kēhāh* for *gēhāh* ! Both words occur only once, and in both places the meaning is disputed. *kēhāh* probably means " relief, lessening of pain ". (151) Regarding *gēhāh* in Prov. 17 : 22, Driver (152) believes that it means " face, appearance ", on the basis of Ar. *ǧihat*[un], " face, aspect ". He compares Prov. 15 : 13, *lēb śāmēaḥ yêṭīb pānîm,* " un coeur heureux fait air riant ", (153) and Prov. 17 : 22, *lēb śāmeaḥ yêṭīb gēhāh,* " un cœur heureux fait mine riante ". (154)

l[e]*šibrekā :* " for your fracture ". Ginsberg (155) compares *UT,* ʿnt : III : 30, *bʿdn ksl tṯbr,* " behind her, her loins do break " ; *UT,* 51 : II : 17-18 ; and *UT,* 125 : 54, with Ezek. 21 : 11-12, where there is mention of *šibrôn motnayim,* " breaking of the loins ".

naḥlāh makkātekā : " your wound is severe ". The parallelism of the phrase with *l*[e]*šibrekā,* matches that in Jer. 10 : 19, *'ôy lî ʿal šibrî //naḥlāh makkātî* ; Jer. 14 : 17, *šeber//makkāh naḥlāh* ; Jer. 30 : 12, *'anûš l*[e]*šibrek//naḥlāh makkātēk.* Hillers (156) sees these texts as being similar in expression to treaty-curses of the " incurable wound ".

ḥlh means " become sick, weak ", but can also be used of " being severely wounded " as in 1 Sam. 31 : 3. In Mari it is found as a Northwest Semitic loanword. A lioness is described as being *šībat u ḫalât,* " old and sick ". (157)

tāq[e]*ʿû kap :* " clap their hands ". Cf. Ps. 47 : 2. Names of parts of the body do not require a suffix. (158)

rāʿāt[e]*kā tāmîd :* " your continuing evil ". This seems to be an example of a construct chain with interposed suffix. (159)

(151) Cf. KB 424b. *HALAT* 175b emends Nah. 3 : 9, *kēhāh* to *gēhāh.*

(152) *ETL* 26 (1950) 344.

(153) *Ibid.*

(154) *Ibid.*

(155) *ANET* 132, n. 18 ; 147, n. 26.

(156) *Treaty-Curses,* pp. 64-66.

(157) *CAD* [Ḫ] 54, *sub ḫalû,* " to be sick ". *HALAT* 303, 305, seems to have overlooked this Mari occurrence.

(158) Cf. Astour, *RHR* 164 (1963) 6, n. 4 ; Dahood, *Psalms I,* p. 89, *passim.*

(159) *Psalms III,* p. 52.

Indices

Index of Subjects

Index of Authors

Index of Biblical Passages

1 Samuel

2 Samuel

1 Kings

2 Kings

Isaiah

Jeremiah

Ezekiel

Job

Proverbs

Canticle of Canticles

Ecclesiastes

Lamentations

Daniel

Nehemiah

Ezra

1 Chronicles

2 Chronicles

Sirach

Index of Ugaritic Passages

Index of Other Northwest Semitic Texts

Index of El Amarna References

Index of Hebrew Words

Index of Ugaritic Words

Index of Other Words

Akkadian

Aramaic

Phoenician-Punic

Syriac